PLANNING TOGETHER

THE ART OF EFFECTIVE TEAMWORK

George Gawlinski and Lois Graessle

Published by
Planning Together Associates

George Gawlinski 281a Wootton Road,
Kings Lynn, Norfolk PE30 3AR UK
Tel +44 (0) 1553 671620
Email: George.Gawlinski@binternet com

Lois Graessle
1 Magnolia Wharf, Strand on the Green
London W4 3NY UK
Tel +44 (0) 181 995 0244
Email: LoisGraessle@compuserve.com

First published 1988
Reprinted with corrections 1989
Reprinted 1990, 1994 & 1996
Reprinted with corrections 1999

Typeset by Cylinder Typesetting Ltd, London

Printed and bound in Great Britain by
Redwood Books, Trowbridge, Wiltshire

British Library Cataloguing in Publication Data

Gawlinski, George
Planning together
1. Management. Team-work. Planning
1. Title 11. Graessle, Lois
658.4'012

ISBN 0-9528577-1-5

CONTENTS

PREFACE

Planning together is a way of helping a team make sense of what it is trying to do and do it effectively.

This book presents a model of planning as a team in nine clear stages, with a choice of activities for each of those stages. It also offers ways of facing up to the conflicts, difficulties and unforeseen events which are always part of the planning process.

Overall, it provides a framework for team-building which is stimulating and challenging, and can even be enjoyable. The consequences of planning in this way may include not only more effective services for users but also a group of individuals who can work together in a more supportive and creative way, even under pressure.

—— WHAT IS A TEAM? ——

We use 'team' to mean people who depend on each other to some extent to get their work done.

—— WHY TEAMS? ——

The basic working unit for many of us is a team, whether that team is one of many at various levels in a large public or private organisation or the sum total of workers in a small voluntary project.

—— WHICH TEAMS? ——

The planning process presented in this book will be of use to a team which is concerned both to deliver a better service or product and also to get satisfaction from working together.

The process has been extensively tested with a wide variety of individuals and teams. Some teams have used this approach to plan their entire workload for three or six months at a time. These have included teams within a major corporation and a project for the single homeless. A group of volunteers used it to plan their charity Christmas card shop. Others have planned a new aspect of their work, such as opening a nursery or neighbourhood advice centre. While the book is aimed particularly at teams, individuals have found parts of the process useful in planning their own work. The authors used it to plan their work on this book.

Your team may be volunteers or a managing committee of a community project; it may be senior managers within a complex public service hierarchy or private sector organisation. The point is that at the end of the day, whatever the nature or size of your organisation, it will be a small group of people who sit down to get something done.

—— WHAT GOES WRONG? ——

Of course, planning goes on already. We have written this book because we have seen, as managers and consultants, how often it goes wrong. Why?

We have found at least part of the answer in some of the ways that teams think about their work, since this affects how they plan, or fail to plan, together. The most common of these ways of thinking are:

UNCLEAR THINKING: thinking is too vague, however worthy, to provide a basis for clear joint working.

ABSENT THINKING: the capacity of some organisations not to plan at all but simply to survive from day to day.

COMMITTEE THINKING: the capacity of some teams to take decisions with which no one is happy, either because of the demand for consensus at all costs or from the need, say, to get to the pub before closing time.

EXPANSION THINKING: an instinct that equates growth, i.e. increases in funding or staffing, with progress. This can lead to a tendency to do anything for which money is available or to make unrealistic promises to funders or consumers.

CHARISMATIC THINKING: letting the enthusiasm of one person blind everyone else to the realities of what they are proposing.

PERSONALITY THINKING: the trap of thinking that all the problems are to do with personality clashes.

SOAPBOX THINKING: the tendency to mistake talking about commitment with putting it into practice.

TREE THINKING: again, an absence of thinking. A team that is too busy to know what it is doing, as in 'we can't see the wood for the trees'.

Do any of these sound familiar?

If so, this book may help you.

We offer an alternative approach that recognises planning as a way of helping a team manage its work and each individual manage themselves.

It can help your team make sound, realistic plans which have a good chance of success. Conflicts, personal needs and feelings, difficulties and unforeseen events here get equal time with setting objectives or assigning tasks. Dealing with them becomes part of the productive process of getting things going, and getting things done.

───── USING THIS BOOK ─────

The model of team planning presented here is a step-by-step process. Each stage follows from the one before. While some of the chapters stand in their own right, such as **3 Taking Stock** and **4 Developing and Sharing a Vision,** the major part of the book's value lies in the fact that it offers a *model* for planning that is coherent and integrated. Therefore, the order is important but not essential.

We suggest that teams take the steps in this order:

INTRODUCING THE MODEL
the stages presented through the experience of a group of friends planning a holiday

DO YOU NEED HELP?
deciding whether you can do this yourselves or whether at some point you might want to bring in someone from outside

TAKING STOCK
taking a realistic look at how things are at present before embarking on planning something new

DEVELOPING AND SHARING A VISION
looking at where you think you are going together

LINKING VALUES, POLICIES AND STRATEGIES
taking the opportunity to consider issues of quality, direction and personal beliefs

PRIORITISING AIMS
agreeing the direction of your work and choosing what to start with

SETTING OBJECTIVES
being clear and specific about what you are aiming to accomplish

GETTING ORGANISED AND STAYING ORGANISED
deciding what has to be done, who will do it and how you will make sure it gets done

EVALUATING PROGRESS
evaluating yourselves for your own benefit and as a way of letting others know what you are doing

The book ends with a final section:

Postscript

HEALTH WARNINGS:
PERSONAL SURVIVAL

This section reminds us that ultimately we have a responsibility to look after ourselves. The postscript offers guidelines to locating sources of stress at work: within the individual, in the team or the organisation as a whole, as well as in the social, political and economic climate. It also reminds us that the management of change can have a profound effect on how we adapt to, or survive, working in a fast-changing environment.

──── USING EACH CHAPTER ────

This book has two major aims:
- ☐ to introduce you to a way of approaching planning as a team
- ☐ to offer you a range of activities which may help you put this model into practice for yourselves

The chapters are designed to meet both these aims. Each chapter follows the same pattern of:

> ### Introduction and Illustrations
> a description of the purpose of the stage with examples drawn from practice

> ### Description of Appropriate Activities
> a brief description of the choice of activities which the team may use in order to work through this stage

> ### Dealing with Common Pitfalls
> Although the process is step by step, planning as a team is unlikely to be straightforward, since we as human beings are not. This section lists the most common hiccups teams seem to encounter at each stage. Sometimes suggestions for solutions or avoidance are offered; in other instances, we simply give an alternative way of seeing the 'problem' – since some 'problems' have no other solution

> ### Activities
> full instructions for timing, resources and briefing for each activity relevant to this stage, as well as samples of any forms that might be used.

──── WHAT ABOUT *TIME?* ────

Is this way of planning as time-consuming as it seems? Yes.

Our experience suggests that the investment of time in planning in this way pays off in more efficient, effective and satisfying work. It saves time previously wasted on bad meetings, unnecessary tasks and the time taken to moan a great deal more.

A small project or team can work through the main chapters (from **3 Taking Stock** to **9 Evaluating Progress**) in two single days or six 3-hour sessions, providing they have no major difficulties in working together or in conceptualising what they want to do.

Teams in more complex situations can usefully be focused on this process in a series of six day-long meetings spread over 6-12 weeks or in a week-long residential course.

Finally it comes down to choice about whether you are willing to risk investing your time as a team in trying to work together more effectively in order to deliver a better service to your users. You take the risk of uncovering uncomfortable realities about how things are at present within your team. You also take the opportunity of doing something about it.

──── LANGUAGE, LABELS AND ──── EXAMPLES ────

We have had to make decisions about the words we use, the kind of examples we select, and the scope of the book.

In speaking of those who are receiving a team's service or product, we have opted to call them users. We felt that this was a more generic term than client, customer, patient or student, understanding that some of you may have other preferences.

This book concentrates on the internal workings of a staff team. As a result, little emphasis is given to relationships with users. Some teams may wish to remedy this by involving users in their planning process, by inviting representatives to planning meetings, by carrying out surveys or interviews or inviting written contributions. **Taking Stock** and **Developing and Sharing a Vision** have been tested as methods of making annual meetings more relevant. Many of the activities allow for sensitive ways of involving users, and volunteers, in what have traditionally been professional debates. We decided, with reluctance, that the scope of this book prevented us from taking this important debate further.

We have tried to use non-sexist language and to avoid culturally-biased examples, to the limits of our own awareness.

Examples are generally drawn from our experience and are biased towards certain kinds of public and voluntary sector activity. We hope none of these factors will mitigate against people using this process in other contexts.

We also recognise that in many instances the lines separating public sector, commercial and voluntary deliveries of services are being eroded. Hence in the examples we have tried to reflect the needs of each.

Whichever context you work in, we hope you can find in this book a way of meeting your own needs as a team.

ACKNOWLEDGEMENTS

The model for team planning presented in this book owes its roots to numerous individuals with whom we have co-worked and to hundreds of individuals who have shared their own experiences through consultancies and training events.

Because of this it is often difficult to know where certain ideas and exercises have originated or been adapted. The book, therefore, represents our own synthesis of many other people's ideas.

Certain individuals have, however, been more closely involved in the development of the book itself. Their support, encouragement and stimulus is reflected throughout. In particular we would like to recognise:

Frankie Armstrong and **Shirley Otto,** who set a direction to our whole way of working and thinking;

Patrick Wright and the Management Unit of the National Council for Voluntary Organisations, both for initiating the book and for supporting its progress so actively, and **Jacqueline Sallon,** our editor at Bedford Square Press;

Piers Worth, who has made comments on the text, both in terms of its clarity and its links to mainstream management theory and literature;

The following who commented on the text at various stages: **Iris Briscoe, Alan Carr, Tim Cook, Christine Holloway, Jo Howard, Bob Hughes, Nick Irving, Simon Keyes, Su Kingsley, Doreen Massey, Shirley Otto** and **Josephine Seccombe;**

Our partners, **Jean Gawlinski** and **Eric Bourne,** for their friendship and good-natured acceptance of the time we have had to spend together.

1
INTRODUCING THE MODEL

We were an assortment of friends and colleagues. Everyone knew everyone else but sometimes only vaguely. I had only met David's wife and Bhavna's husband at parties.

DECEMBER Taking Stock
In fact, when we got down to it at Sue's we discovered just how little we knew about each other. Some of us were well off, some were clearly struggling. We liked very different things. It became obvious straightaway that Sharon and Mike did not really intend to go through with it. I think they decided financial solvency was their priority this year.

DECEMBER Developing and Sharing a Vision
Those of us who were still committed to the idea met the next week to talk about what we really wanted out of a holiday. We shared horror stories about the holidays we had hated and fantasised about the one we might have. At this point, lots of sunshine and good food were the only points on which we agreed.

Neither planning nor teamwork are the exclusive preserve of management training and experience, although many of us are put off because we have been led to think they are. Each of us who grows up in a family, plays in a sports team, runs a jumble sale or organises a babysitting rota knows something about teamwork. Each if us who prepares for exams, redecorates a room or arranges a holiday knows something about planning.

The following story will illustrate the way planning is approached in this book. The holiday example is being used because it is not related to your work but to the process by which you work. The point of this chapter is to introduce the steps in this approach to planning. Examples from work will be included in later chapters.

This account of what happened to a group of friends is told by Jean, one of the women in the group. Although the names have been changed, the story in spirit is true.

NOVEMBER Developing and Sharing a Vision
One night in the pub the idea of taking a holiday together was floated amongst a group of us. It was mid-winter and the thought of sunshine brought out a great deal of enthusiasm.

The idea still appealed the next time we met, so we agreed we had to talk seriously about what it might involve before it was too late. We decided to have supper one night at Sue's so that she would not have a problem about a babysitter.

JANUARY Linking Values, Policies and Strategies
It was also clear that we would have to learn to adapt to each other. For instance, we had eight children amongst us. You could tell from the way people talked that we all had different attitudes towards children. I was not sure we could reconcile them. Raj and Bhavna were clearly more strict than David and Miriam; Sue as a single parent would need more babysitting support; my own two were teenagers, which might cause problems for some of the others.

JANUARY Prioritising Aims

All of the women were adamant that we wanted a holiday where we did not have to cook all the time. We tried to make the point that we wanted a holiday for us as well as for everyone else.

Anyway, by the end of the evening we felt a lot closer. Most of us decided that we were really serious about the holiday venture. David and Miriam dropped out at this point. I knew they had been having problems between themselves. They weren't the only ones who could do without having their relationships examined at close quarters, but the rest of us still seemed game. I know there was some feeling about sexual boundaries, with Sue on her own. We didn't really talk about this directly, and we liked Sue so much that it didn't seem a major issue.

FEBRUARY Setting Objectives

At this point we finally got down to the details. It was early February by now and we needed to get on with it.

We knew we all wanted sunshine abroad but from that point we had a hundred different ideas. First choice was four weeks in a hotel on the beach in the Seychelles. We started at the fantasy end of things! No one had that much holiday except Carla, who teaches, and none of us had that kind of money.

Finally, after we came to terms with our finances and the children's needs and the time available, the Seychelles dream turned into 10 days camping in Brittany in late August. It was also clear we had other criteria: access to sailing; take-out eating places and a laundrette within walking distance; a disco within reach but not within hearing.

MARCH Getting Organised and Staying Organised

Then we got down to the business of organisation. Carla's partner, Winston, offered to get everything sorted out. It was tempting but we knew we had to share out jobs. We were all busy and we did not want to lumber one person with the whole thing. We decided what needed to be done by when, and then set times when we would meet and check progress. We didn't want a crisis because someone had forgotten the tickets or tents and no one knew until the day before. We also talked about what to do if something went wrong with the plans while we were away or if we fell out with each other.

APRIL Evaluating Progress

I had a particularly heavy spring at work; also my mother was seriously ill. I was glad of the Tuesday night meetings that chased us up and provided lists of duties. Otherwise I suspect that I would have failed to do my bit, or never have had a holiday this year.

The practice camping weekend was a disaster. We hoped the philosophy of 'bad dress rehearsal, good performance' applied to holidays as well.

SEPTEMBER Evaluating Our Experience

Oh, yes, the holiday. It was a lot of fun, the most relaxing I've ever had, I think. Even my teenagers loved it, and they don't love much at the moment. They liked having familiar people around who weren't their parents. The combination of doing your own thing while having friends nearby, and other people for the children to be with, seemed to suit everyone.

When we met after the holiday to talk about it, most of us were commenting on how much fun the preparation was as well. Not only did we get a good holiday out of it, we also had some good times on those Tuesday nights when we got together to do the planning.

———— ACTIVITIES ————

The story above shows how one group of friends planned their holiday.

Activity 1 Personal Planning Styles offers an easy way for you as a team to approach joint planning by sharing your experiences of holidays and how you have planned them. This should make you alert to the issues involved without getting stuck on the details of your work at this point.

ACTIVITY 1
PERSONAL PLANNING STYLES

'I thought everyone else shared my passion for clear targets, endless lists and lots of meetings. It took some months and a number of strained relationships before I realised that other people found this way of working killed their sense of creativity and fun.'

Aims

a. to start the process of working together

b. to extract issues about individuals' personal planning styles

c. to see what effect these might have on the team's future work

Timing

1 hour:

       10 minutes to read and think individually

       20 minutes in pairs

       30 minutes in small groups (8)

Resources needed

- a copy of chapter 1: Introducing the Model, for each participant
- a room where participants can work in pairs, in small groups 8 and together (if the team is larger than 8)
- a facilitator to keep time and lead group discussion.

——— BRIEFING ———

1. Explain the aims of the session to participants, reminding them that while the subject may seem frivolous, our own style of planning at home often matches that at work. Emphasise that there is not a right or wrong way of doing things. This is not a test. They need not share material that is sensitive or confidential.

2. Allow each participant 10 minutes to read the story of planning a holiday in chapter 1 and then think about how they planned a recent holiday of their own. If anyone has not taken a holiday recently, ask them to think about how they plan or approach their weekends, leave, or leisure time.

3. Ask participants to select a partner and work in pairs for 20 minutes, each person taking 5 minutes in turn to describe how they planned a recent holiday. Then as a pair take 10 minutes to discuss what they learnt about their own and each other's planning style.

4. Participants then reform as a group (or in groups of no more than 8 each). One person agrees to act as a facilitator. Each person then feeds back (in under 2 minutes) two things they learnt about their own planning styles from this exercise, e.g.

'I like to plan things methodically in great detail, well in advance of the event. I can feel ill if this does not happen.'

'By the time my holidays start, I am usually drowning in lists and would prefer to stay at home and have a rest.'

'I always seem to end up doing what other people want and usually don't enjoy my holidays.'

5. The facilitator then helps the group to look at any issues that have emerged which may affect the work of the team, e.g.

We all seem to hate planning.

We all worry that too much planning may kill creativity.

6. These should be listed on a piece of chart paper and displayed so that the whole group can use them as a reference during the rest of the planning process.

Any serious issues, like 'none of us believe in planning', might need to be addressed before going any further **Activity 12 Facing the Facts: Examining the Implications** might be particularly helpful if you have reached this point.

2
DO YOU NEED HELP?

In order to plan together as a team you have to meet together as a team. For each of these meetings you need someone to help you keep to the task and to the time and to help you over difficulties in working together.

The group of friends planning a holiday together were lucky, as Jean acknowledged:

'Two of us were particularly good at making sure that everyone got their say and that at the end of our Tuesday night meetings things were clear. I had a thing about keeping notes, so I used an old roll of lining paper to keep a record of who was doing what, and Phil, for all his casual style, kept us to the point even when there were distractions, like food and drink.'

This does not always happen, having members who can help the group work together. If there had not been anyone, a good travel agent might have helped sort out many of the things they did for themselves. Or they might have had the bad luck of using a travel agent who thought he or she knew best and sold them a holiday they did not really want.

Teams wanting to plan all or part of their work together face the same dilemma. **Who will help each meeting achieve its aims in the time available, in terms of both the tasks to be done and the way in which the team works together?**

You may choose one person either from within the team or from outside to fill this role or you may want to take it in turns, only calling in an outsider for particularly demanding or stressful sessions.

Whoever you choose must be able to remain neutral, while helping others to contribute their own ideas; and to help the group keep to the task yet be able to call a halt if the tone of the meeting becomes obstructive or destructive.

The person playing such a role, whether from within your team or outside it, is usually called a facilitator, although the French term, *animateur*, seems more warmly descriptive.

It is easier if the team leader does not also have to be the facilitator. It can be more helpful to the team and satisfying to the team leader if she or he is free to contribute their ideas and information rather than to oversee the dynamics of the meeting as well. But for any number of reasons, you may not find it possible to divide the two tasks. Teams have different experiences of dealing with this:

Team 1

'As team leader I wanted to bring in a consultant so that I could be free to participate in our planning as an equal. Things were so bad between Ned and me at this time that he would not trust my choice of consultant, and I guess if I am honest, I would not have trusted his choice either. So what I did was to go to the consultant on my own and learn what I needed to do, then take the team through it myself. It worked amazingly well. I had a lot more confidence in being able to get us to where we needed to go, and that helped me finally to face up to our difficulties with each other.'

Team 2

'Something went wrong in our team. We are working as a collective but no one was willing to come forward and take responsibility for facilitating meetings, even when we knew they had the skills and used them in other places. Everyone preferred to have a consultant. At the end of the series we decided we would ask her to run some training sessions on facilitating meetings, so that in the future we could do it for ourselves. We could not afford a consultant every time, and in any case it is something we should be able to do.'

You may find it helpful to ask yourselves:

1. Is there anyone, or several of you, whom you would all feel happy with as having the skills and in whom the group feels confidence? If not,

2. Is there someone closely connected with your team, such as a member of your management committee or a worker from another organisation, who could help you on time-for-time basis or just because they are willing to help out? If not,

3. Will you need to go into the professional consultant/facilitator network?

If your answer was 'no' to **1** and **2** and 'yes' to **3,** you will have to pay well to get a good facilitator, so it is worth being very clear what you want. Do you want an expert in your field, say homelessness or child abuse or housing benefits? Or do you want an expert facilitator who also has some familiarity with your field?

If you go for the expert in your field you need to be clear whether you are asking them to guide you through the complexities of the process while you make the decisions or whether they are coming to advise you.

If they are coming to advise you as well as facilitating, do you know the difference? What provision will you set up for telling them you do not like what they suggest? It is hard for anyone, whether team leader or outside consultant, to wear two hats in facilitating team planning. If you want advice, it may be helpful to turn that need into a training day in its own right and separate it from the planning process.

Given the cost of good facilitators, as well as the value in learning these skills yourselves, you may be wiser to try to do the bulk of the facilitating yourselves and only call in an outsider for crucial blocks or stages. In particular the beginning for taking stock and the point when the team gets blocked at any stage are places where an outsider can bring useful insights. Unblocking things is what facilitators do best.

No one in fact is a good facilitator in the abstract. There will be those who suit your team and others with whom some of you simply do not feel comfortable, even if you do not understand why. The best way of finding someone with whom you have a good chance of working well is to ask around similar teams to see whether they can recommend somebody. Alternatively, ring one of the national organisations related to your work. Most facilitator-consultants get all their work by word-of-mouth and do not advertise. They are usually very busy, so think well ahead.

Consider clearly how you will judge them to be 'successful'. Brief them and hold them to that.

ACTIVITIES

Activity 2 Getting Help offers you a way of identifying what you need from a facilitator.

DEALING WITH COMMON PITFALLS

Free-for-all
Some teams, especially those working non-hierarchically or collectively, are wary of someone dominating the process and so do not want to have a facilitator at all. The answer to their concerns may be to have each group member take it in turn to facilitate a session, perhaps preceding this with training for all members of the team in the skills of facilitating and chairing meetings. This may help to reinforce the point about facilitation, which is to enable each member of a group to contribute, an aim that strongly supports the principles of non-hierarchical and collective working.

The guru syndrome
Watch yourselves for the danger of expecting a facilitator to be a guru who will come and solve all your problems. Watch your facilitator if she or he seems to have come bringing this tendency with them. A facilitator will help you to identify and face your own problems, which leads on to

Facing the unthinkable: saying the unsaid
You may actually want someone to come and confront you with reality because you cannot see it or are unable to face this for yourselves. If this happens, thank them, do not kick them.

ACTIVITY 2
GETTING HELP

'This has been the most successful planning day we have had together for the last six years. You've helped us talk together as a team, clarify our own ideas, and develop confidence in our own abilities. Thank you again.'

Aim
to provide a framework within which a team can make decisions about getting outside help

Timing
1-2 hours:
20-30 minutes in pairs
40-90 minutes in groups

Resources needed
whiteboard or chart paper
checklist: 'Getting Help'

——— BRIEFING ———

1 Staff work in pairs initially to interview each other on their feelings and views about getting help with their planning meetings.

2 One person agrees to act as a facilitator and leads the group through the checklist.

3 Final decision is recorded on whiteboard or chart paper.

——— CHECKLIST ——— ——— FOR ——— ——— GETTING ——— ——— HELP ———

1 Do you organise facilitation from within the team?

2 Does the team leader facilitate or do you come to some other arrangement?

3 Is there someone available from a similar agency or another team in the organisation who could facilitate free for you or on a time-for-time basis?

4 List possible people who could be approached and agree who will approach them.

5 If you are proposing to hire a professional facilitator/consultant, do you want:

a a facilitator

b a facilitator with familiarity in your field

c a consultant who is an 'expert' in your field but who will also facilitate your discussion and decision making

d a consultant who is an 'expert' and whom you are buying in for advice and guidance?

6 If you decide to hire a consultant, consider carefully how you will consider them to be successful. List your criteria.

7 How much time can you devote to working with a consultant?

8 What can you afford to pay?

9 Who is available – or how can you find out who is available?

10 Who will decide which suggested consultant-facilitators to approach (and interview, if you have decided to do this)?

your team leader

the entire team

team representatives.

11 Who will agree the final contract with the consultant?

your team leader

the entire team

team representatives.

12 Decide whether this will be

in person

on the phone

in writing.

13 Complete the checklist by

briefing the consultant carefully

confirming arrangements in writing

holding them to the contract or renegotiating it if you discover it is no longer appropriate.

3
TAKING STOCK

Yet for other teams, the resistance can be enormous. Perhaps it is because we see work a bit like a river. It just keep flowing, the load sometimes heavier, sometimes lighter but never drying up. New work joins in the flow almost unnoticed. Perhaps we are afraid that if we are not in there paddling, the flow of work will pass us by.

The soundest first step in planning for the future is to stand still and check how things are at present – with each individual, between team members, and with the work itself.

Pause and reflect on the holiday example, to illustrate the impact of taking stock.

When the group of friends floated the idea of taking a holiday together, they talked about their present circumstances before going any further. Did people need to have a holiday quickly or later? How were their bank balances? Were there any family commitments, like sick relatives, that might make planning difficult? What about work? Could they take time off at roughly the same times or did someone have a big project coming to a crucial stage at just the time everyone else was free? What were relationships like in the group? (If Phil and Raj were still at loggerheads, it might prejudice the holiday.) And what about David and Miriam, who were thinking of splitting up?

They had all agreed that they needed a holiday, except for Sharon and Mike who dropped out early on. But was there any particular reason why they should take a holiday together? They stopped and asked that question. Good reasons might have been common interests, or economy, or just liking being together. Here, all three answers applied, so there were significant gains to be made by their planning a holiday together.

The stage of stopping to review and take stock can seem like common sense if it is part of how your team regularly works together. Like the necessity of breathing in after breathing out.

If we choose to pull over to the side and pause on the bank, we might ask ourselves questions such as

- is our boat leaking?
- can we carry on or do we need to stop for major repairs?
- is everyone paddling flat out or is there some slack in our 'crew'?
- is the river itself changing course – or drying up?
- are there any obstacles ahead that we need to be aware of?

Is it possible that the prospect of having to ask and answer these questions is in fact the problem? Asking them may mean that you get answers you do not like or do not know what to do with. Most of us like to avoid that reality most of the time.

Yet what you do with the answers is really up to you. Two teams can come up with the same answer and choose to deal with it in a different way. Both the teams quoted below had stopped to review their work, before considering taking on a new area of work. Both teams discovered that each member of their team was overloaded with work already. They chose to do two different things with this conclusion:

Team 1

We were all excited about this new project. The review really faced us with the fact of how severe our current overload was. Reluctantly we decided that it was much more important for us to face up to this, as it had been a recurring theme for ages, than to jump into another new project. We set ourselves a time limit and a way of dealing with the overload, so that it does not become an excuse to say 'no' to everything.

Team 2

Although it was clear that we were already overworked, none of us could bear to miss the opportunity to take on this counselling project in collaboration with the NHS. We had been wanting this sort of collaboration for years. We decided to accept short-term overload but to monitor ourselves at each stage, to see if we could underpin our enthusiasm with reality. We are going to look for a team consultant for a short time, to help us get started on this.

ACTIVITIES

There are many ways to approach a team review. The route you choose will depend on what your concern is at the moment, how long you have worked together, how much time you are willing to set aside and the way in which you like to work. A review, of whatever length, needs to include:

- checking how individuals are;
- asking how the team is working together;
- looking at current work in light of your aims and of feedback from your users.

It does not matter where you start, so long as you end up knowing how people are feeling, as well as what they are doing individually and jointly.

An assortment of activities may be of use for this purpose:

CHECKING OUT INDIVIDUALS

Activity 3: Your Working Week provides data that will be of use throughout the planning process. It will help each individual to know how they are spending their time and whether their feelings, for example of either overload or underutilisation, are reflected in their diaries, filofaxes or time manager systems.

Activity 4: Achievements and Frustrations leads you to reach conclusions about the team and the organisation of which it is a part by building on the achievements and frustrations of each individual worker.

Where a feeling of stress and unhappiness seems pervasive and the general tone of the team is pale grey, **Activity 5: Checking for Burnout** may be the first step.

CHECKING OUT TEAM RELATIONSHIPS

Particularly in teams where many members are new or new to each other, a good foundation for looking at working patterns and working styles can be built using **Activity 6: Sharing Idiosyncracies.**

Are your team meetings a joke or a bore? Do they wind you up for the rest of the week? **Activity 7: Looking At Your Meetings** offers a practical way of exploring the dynamics and developing the skills involved in meetings.

LOOKING AT THE WORK

Are you delivering services effectively? **Activity 8: Do-It-Yourself Consultancy** outlines conditions for delivering services effectively and allows you to measure your team's work.

Activity 9: Star Chart: Mapping Relationships is a way of looking at the quality of the relationships with everyone who is involved with or affects your work.

LOOKING AT EVERYTHING AT ONCE

An alternative to starting with a specific focus is to structure ways of people sharing their concerns across the board.

Activity 10: Active Listening shows how to set up structures for listening carefully and helping each other to identify issues and concerns.

Activity 11: Setting A Team Agenda is a procedure for mapping out the team's concerns ranging from philosophy to practice.

WHAT DO YOU DO WITH THE OUTCOMES?

A review will leave the team with an immense amount of information, some of which may be acutely uncomfortable. **Activity 12: Facing the Facts: Examining the Implications** will help you order this information then move on to do something about it.

If one of the outcomes is that you finally acknowledge that you are in quite a mess, returning to **Activity 2: Getting Help** may be the most constructive next step.

At this stage you may want to move on to **Activity 13: Sorting Out Who Does What** in order to make sure what you are going to do with the outcomes and who is going to do it.

DEALING WITH COMMON PITFALLS

The danger of stopping to take stock of what you are doing and how you are feeling about it is that you might get answers that are uncomfortable. The most common pitfalls relate to this:

Not taking time at all
Some individuals and some organisations either pride themselves on being too busy to stop or have a feeling that taking time out for reflection and review

is self-indulgent. In fact, there is no way to gauge whether what you are doing meets the needs of your users and other workers, not to mention yourself, if you do not take the time to stop and ask. If you are hoping to be an innovative and responsive service, then you need to stop and look at what you are doing.

Talking in generalisations
Often team members are wary about reviewing because of bad experiences in the past. These may have included general discussions that seemed to get nowhere, reviews that felt like inquisitions, or where your own work was passed over. The stages presented in this chapter are designed to make reviewing more satisfactory for all involved. Each individual is given equal time, which also allows discussion to be rooted in what is really happening in the team, rather than floating into vague territory.

Carpet sweeping
Teams often have a tendency to fudge or hide issues or feelings under the carpet. This can be because the team has no way of dealing with feelings; because there is an unstated, or even explicit, agreement that

such feelings are not relevant to the work; or because an individual believes that she is the only one feeling that way and is afraid to raise it.

If difficult issues and feelings are avoided at this stage, there is the real danger that vital information may be missed out. Feelings such as anger at the way a reorganisation is being handled, guilt about how users are being treated, or serious animosity between two team members are just as valid as information on the amount of the budget or the allocation of holidays.

The facilitator needs to have the confidence and skill, as well as the team's permission, to help the team face anything that is interfering with their effective work and working. The key ingredient is whether the person who is facilitating this stage feels able to handle difficult issues of this sort. If not, he or she needs to make this clear to the team, then help them decide what to do next, such as bringing in a consultant to help.

Ignoring messages
Reviews leave a team with many messages about its general well-being or malaise. Yet many of us have a tendency to plough on with the new work or new project, regardless of the messages. The facilitator can help a team by being particularly rigorous in asking, 'Can you carry on or do you need to stop for urgent repairs?' As this stage comes at the end of the review, it can be tempting just to let it slide. Joint vigilance is necessary.

Boundaries
Many workers are afraid of reviewing because they fear they will be expected and pushed to reveal personal things that they feel are no one's business at work. You are reviewing together because you work together. It is important that even in the more personal elements of taking stock both the facilitator and group members are clear about the boundaries between your working lives and your personal lives outside work. This kind of work requires a difficult balance between personal openness when that is related to work and protection of privacy when it is not. Individuals need to feel reasonably confident that they are secure from invasion of privacy, protected from attack, and that difficult issues will be dealt with sensitively.

Choices
The hard fact about making choices is that if you choose to do one set of things you are often choosing not to do another. You need to be aware of this. For example, one team was offered more money for more staff for a new MSC scheme. They started trying to plan for this new scheme. Instead the facilitator helped them to face the question of whether they

should be taking on more staff or schemes at a point when all team members were sensing a loss of direction and quality in their current work. Is it, for you, the time for expansion or consolidation? What are you choosing to neglect or discard by taking on a new area of work?

Not forgetting praise

The current fashion in teamwork is for giving honest feedback. There is a tendency to think this means critical feedback. A crucial part of a team review is to look at achievements and to give recognition for them. One team had worked above and beyond the call of duty or contractual obligations to keep a service going during a difficult period. They had enjoyed the challenge of working like that, the satisfaction of giving any service at all, and often good service, while the whole organisation was in a state of chaos. But they were left bitter at the end of it. Why? 'Not one of the principal officers ever came in and said "thank you" or "well done".' Another group of team leaders went to the opposite extreme. They set as a target, 'give praise to everyone at least once a day'. Not surprisingly, their team members felt this was not spontaneous or genuine and gave them a hard time about it until they changed their approach.

ACTIVITY 3
YOUR WORKING WEEK

'I was shocked when I realised that I was routinely committed to working an average of 60 hours a week and that my employers now took this for granted. No wonder staff tended to leave after only 18 months.'

Aims
a. to help individuals review their present working commitments
b. to explore how clear an understanding individuals have of priorities within their work.

Timing
1½ hours:
45 minutes individually
45 minutes in group discussion

Resources needed
felt pens

two sheets of chart paper for each individual

a room with space on the walls to display the charts

a facilitator to keep time and lead group discussion

BRIEFING

Start with an actual week's work, last week if you were at work, so that you can remember the details well. Take it in the following steps:

1 List all the jobs you did, formal, e.g. attending a committee meeting; or informal, e.g. helping the secretary stuff envelopes to get the mailing out on time.

2 Go back and list as near as possible how much time each job took. If you discover areas of work or pockets of time you forgot to include initially, add them in and make a mental note to wonder why you forgot them in the first place.

3 Add up the number of hours you actually worked that week and write the sum down.

No week is average, but in order to get a more general idea of your workload, go through this exercise again.

4 List all the regular jobs you do in an average week, adding any that you did not do in the first week you chose but which are regular.

5 Go through the list and by each activity roughly estimate the average amount of time you spend each week on it. (If you only do something once a year for a week, for instance your annual report or performance reviews, divide the number of hours you give to the task that week by 52; if you do it once a month, divide it by four in order to give you the weekly average).

Do not worry too much about being precise. This is a very rough guide. On the other hand, do not omit things because you think you 'should not' be doing them or you are working 'too hard'.

6 Add up the number of committed hours you have in a week.

Experience suggests that between 25 and 30 hours of *committed* time a week is reasonable. If this exercise comes out at more than 30, there is the risk that you are overloaded with work; 40-50 means that almost certainly this is the case.

7 Check these figures against how you are actually feeling. Are you feeling under a great deal of pressure or, alternatively, very challenged? Are you working very long hours? Do you feel you have something to show for it or that you do not know where the time goes? Are there many jobs not getting done properly?

8 As a team, compare notes on what you each discovered about your workloads. Note on a large sheet of paper any points that are common ones.

9 For the time being, just hold on to these points. You will need to refer back to them at the end of the planning process, when you are testing the reality of your plans.

ACTIVITY 4
ACHIEVEMENTS AND FRUSTRATIONS

'It's been a hard year with many disappointments and frustrations over finance and staffing. Yet much to my surprise we've managed to set up several new and successful projects, I introduced a new staffing structure and fought off closure.'

Aim
To take stock in a personal and informal way of individual feelings about their work during the past year.

Timing
1 hour:
20 minutes in pairs
40 minutes in group discussion

Resources needed
chart paper, bluetack, felt pens
space to work both as a group and for individuals to work in pairs
facilitator to keep time and to lead group discussion

———— BRIEFING ————

1 Work initially in pairs, each in turn interviewing the other. Ask your partner to list
a. three achievements
b. three frustrations
in doing their job in the past year, e.g.
a. surviving;
    recruiting an extra staff member;
    getting a grant from the XYZ Trust.
b. constant staff sickness;
    insensitive senior management during wage negotiations;
    inadequate office conditions.
Encourage your partner to give examples when the point is general.

2 Ask your partner whether their energy level at work at the moment is high, medium or low, and if you have the time, enquire why this is so.

3 The facilitator takes feedback from each individual about their partner's achievements and frustrations, and energy levels. This is listed on chart paper for everyone to see.

4 Using the information on the chart as a basis, discuss as a group what the points reveal about
■ the quality of your teamwork
■ the state of your organisation
■ the quality of your services
■ the major common problems
■ the major common successes
■ the circumstances the team is working in and
■ the pressures affecting it from the outside, e.g.
a. we are all very tired and have low energy;
b. the poor office accommodation is getting us all down;
c. we created a number of successful new products last year in spite of all the factors going against us;
d. clients say they got a good service.

5 List any points that team members feel need further attention; decide who is going to have responsibility for taking each of them forward and by when.

ACTIVITY 5
CHECKING FOR BURNOUT

'I'd read about burnout, but never thought it would happen to me until I realised that I was coping with increased work pressure by drinking more alcohol, never taking proper holidays and finding it impossible to delegate.'

Aim
to increase awareness both for the team and the individual of the possibility of burnout.

Timing
45 minutes:
15 minutes for individuals to fill in checklist
30 minutes for discussion

Resources needed
one copy of **Burnout Checklist** for each individual
facilitator to lead group discussion and keep time

—— BRIEFING ——

1 Each individual fills in checklist, confidentially and only for their own information. You may wish to mark yourself on a scale of 1 (low) to 5 (high). Total your score when you have completed the checklist.

2 Draw a horizontal line on a blackboard or piece of chart paper and list individual totals along the line, ranging from 18 on the left to 90 on the right. Do not list individual names with scores.

3 Discuss as a group how much burnout is or may be a feature of the team's work. If an individual or most members of the team score high, you have a real issue and serious attention needs to be given to overload.

4 If burnout has been shown to be a relevant issue for the team, list possible ways of dealing with it.

Burnout Checklist

You may wish to mark yourself down the left-hand margin on a scale of 1 (low) to 5 (high), then total the numbers when you have completed the list.

1 Not sleeping well at night.

2 Feeling low in energy all day.

3 Not able to concentrate on work.

4 Not able to listen attentively to colleagues or clients.

5 Postponing work, visits, meetings.

6 Exceptionally tired after work.

7 Frequent colds or flu or back trouble.

8 Easily upset by other people's comments, whether made directly or indirectly.

9 Suspicion of everyone else's intentions.

10 Increasing use of alcohol (or other drugs) at lunchtimes and immediately after work.

11 Frequent headaches.

12 A sense of failure.

13 Not wanting to go to work.

14 Conflict at home with partner and/or family.

15 Frequent absences from work.

16 Increasing working-to-rule.

17 Loss of positive feelings towards users.

18 Strong resistance to any change in working conditions.

ACTIVITY 6
SHARING IDIOSYNCRACIES

'Halfway up a mountain or in the middle of some crucial negotiations is not the best time to find out that someone can't stand heights or work well in meetings that go on after 8 pm.'

Aim

to get to know each other's preferences and idiosyncracies prior to working together.

Timing

1 hour:
10 minutes on own
20 minutes in pairs
10 minutes reading posters
20 minutes in group discussion

Resources needed

felt pens
chart paper
bluetack, wall space to display charts
facilitator to keep time and lead group discussion

BRIEFING
---

1 Select a group facilitator to keep time and lead group discussion at the end.

2 Each individual spends 10 minutes alone writing down on a scrap of paper three things that you think it would be helpful for colleagues to know about you – things that wind you up, your style of anger, working habits, your favourite approach to work meetings, e.g.

– 'If I am angry I tend to go off in a corner and sulk, so leave me alone for a while. Eventually I come back and deal with the issue.'

– 'I need a cup of coffee before starting work or speaking to anyone in the mornings.'

– 'If I don't know someone well I can appear rather formal and competitive.'

– 'I like meetings to be short and to the point, otherwise I get impatient and bad tempered.'

– 'I'm scared of public speaking – and would prefer to avoid it.'

3 Individuals select a partner and take 20 minutes to discuss and clarify what they have written and then write down on a large sheet of chart paper those things that they are willing to share with the rest of the group. Make sure their names are at the top. As a variation, each might want to design a logo with their initials.

4 Everyone displays their charts – and everyone takes 10 minutes to walk around and read each other's.

5 The facilitator convenes the group again to discuss what they have learnt from the charts that might influence the way they work together in both a positive and a negative sense, e.g.

– 'I'm glad to know someone else is bad tempered first thing in the morning.'

– 'I'm glad to know that Mary admits to getting bad tempered under pressure – I always thought it was something I had done.'

– 'I recognise that Jack needs to smoke while he is working – but I find it impossible to work in the same room. Is he prepared to consider doing without cigarettes at work?'

6 Note issues that need resolving in future discussion or action. Agree who does what, by when or the date and time for further discussion.

ACTIVITY 7
LOOKING AT YOUR MEETINGS

'Their meetings, when they happened, and it wasn't often, were like reruns of long forgotten wars. No one knew why they happened this way, just that it was the tradition. As a result, no important decisions ever got made in meetings.'

Aim

to give a team the chance to review the quality of their meetings.

Timing

1–2 hours:

20 minutes in pairs

40-100 minutes in group

Resources needed

whiteboard, flip chart or chart paper

felt pens

facilitator to keep time and lead group discussion

——— BRIEFING ———

1 Individuals work in pairs for 20 minutes to interview each other about their feelings on how meetings are organised and run in their team, and in any other setting in their organisation in which they all take part in meetings. They might ask the following questions:

a. how do we make decisions, e.g. majority, consensus, team leader or other member of senior staff?

b. how do we record what we are doing and who does this?

c. what do we do when things start going wrong and the meetings are ineffective or unpleasant or uncomfortable?

d. how long are our meetings, on average?

e. what different kinds of meetings do we have?

f. how much time do we spend in meetings

   (i)   talking to no real purpose;

   (ii) sharing information;

   (iii) concentrating on important decisions;

   (iv) talking about how we are feeling about work and about working with each other?

2 The facilitator then leads a group discussion, collating and charting the main points that have emerged from discussions in pairs.

3 The group brainstorms, throwing out ideas initially without censorship or discussion, about how to improve their meetings.

4 From this list, the group identifies areas of agreement and disagreement, then agrees a list of common ground rules for running the meetings. Try to reach a consensus but if at the end of the meeting you have not been able to, agree to a majority vote.

Ground rules (samples)

No smoking but breaks every hour

Arrange for telephone calls to be diverted

Interruptions only in emergencies

Start and end promptly

Chair to use skills to ensure equal participation by all.

---

5 Agree how you will monitor yourselves to test for progress or backsliding in your meetings, e.g. taking 10 minutes for review at the end of each meeting; having a review of the state of your meetings every three or six months.

ACTIVITY 8
DO-IT-YOURSELF CONSULTANCY

'Many organisations bring in expensive consultants who only tell them what everyone knows already and are afraid to say to each other.'

Aim

to help team members identify to what degree your organisation meets basic criteria for delivering services effectively.

Timing

1 hour:
15 minutes individually
45 minutes to chart and discuss

Resources needed

copy of selected checklists, for each individual
chart paper and felt tip pens
facilitator to keep time and lead discussion

—————— BRIEFING ——————

The checklists are service-industry biased. If this is not appropriate for your team, change the wording to suit your own expression. The forms might be used in the following way:

1 Give each member of the team a copy of the checklist and ask them to rate how they assess the organisation.

2 The facilitator should note the checklist headings on a large sheet of paper on a stand or the wall and mark beside each heading the number each individual ranked each item. (It will take approximately two minutes per person to read off numbers. Make it clear that there is to be no discussion at this stage.)

3 Once all the rankings have been noted, look at those with either consistently high or consistently low markings, or where an individual has marked high or low, and discuss the reasons for the rankings. (Allow at least half an hour but no more than 45 minutes for this step.)

4 If the facilitator and group would find it helpful, take a separate sheet of paper and make a summary of the main positive points and the main points of concern which have been identified.

5 Be clear at this stage whether the group is empowered to make decisions for action arising from any of these points or to make recommendations to a formal team meeting. Agree and take whatever action is appropriate before closing the session.

Find out what you are not doing but should be. Assess your team and/or organisation, yourself as a worker, and your relationships to your users. Use a rating of 1 (low) to 5 (acceptable) to 10 (above average) for the points listed below. Note situations, examples, or issues that come to mind as you do the rating.

CONDITIONS————— RATING ————— NOTES—————

organisational

1 Has the agency researched and understood user need?

2 Are its goals and working methods clear?

3 Are other people, especially users, clear about what service/s the organisation is offering?

4 Are staffing levels adequate?

5 Is recruitment and training effective?

6 Are workers well supervised and supported?

7 Are working conditions adequate and appropriate to the tasks?

8 Are local services co-ordinated and planned effectively?

9 Does some agreement exist vis-à-vis working methods and core philosophy?

10 Do agencies and organisations who have to work together trust and respect each other's work?

user/worker

1 Do workers make clear assessments of need?

2 Are both users and workers clear as to the goals of intervention, the time scale and the working methods?

3 Is the intervention being used appropriate to what the user needs/wants?

4 Are workers skilled, knowledgeable and experienced?

5 Is long-term support available for those who need it?

6 Can the user move between related agencies and organisations without his or her confidence or progress being disrupted?

CONSULTANCY CHECKLIST B:
COMMON BARRIERS TO GOOD PRACTICE

Find your pet hate. Rate your own team, agency or organisation on a scale of 1 (low) to 5 (average) to 10 (high), according to how closely the descriptions match your experience. Note any issues or examples that arise for you during the marking.

BARRIERS AND DESCRIPTION	RATING	NOTES
1 Politics Central government is confused or ambivalent about services, i.e. expects much, gives too little, changes mind often.		
2 Policy and Planning There is an absence of agreed policy about services at a national, regional or local level; investment in buildings, people and services is haphazard.		
3 Professional Different professional groups are competing for power, mystique, status, collectively devaluing users' needs, views, opinions.		
4 People Managers, planners, researchers, fieldworkers are personally uncommitted, disenchanted, tired, cynical.		
5 Practice Working methods are ill-defined, research findings are ignored and no good theoretical basis for the work exists.		
6 Training Training is poor or non-existent.		

Find your own agency. Rate your organisation, agency or project on a scale of 1 (low) to 5 (high) according to how closely each description describes your organisation. Note examples that affected your rating or issues which you would like to discuss.

ORGANISATIONAL MODELS — RATINGS — NOTES

1 Nominalists
A caring organisation in name only. Typically this organisation cares very little for its customers or users; essentially it is concerned with itself.

2 Entrepreneurs
An agency that keeps taking on new things; gets excited by constant innovation; neglects settled routine work.

3 Trendies
An organisation that keeps changing with the latest fashion, be it good or bad.

4 Professionals
An organisation that is more interested in the development of professional expertise than in the needs of users.

5 Antagonists
An organisation in which polarity, anger and resentment have become the dominant theme.

ORGANISATIONAL MODELS	RATINGS	NOTES
6 Newlyweds A new project or agency which becomes absorbed in the beauty of the new agency; exuding friendship, focusing on homebuilding activities, and often naive about the future.		
7 Sell-Outs A project or agency which aims at the biggest grant at the risk of being owned spiritually and financially by funders. Such an organisation is often no longer master of itself and its direction.		
8 Expansionists An organisation with a motto such as, '300% growth this year', judging itself by expansion, then celebrating until it is in over its head, often funding last year's deficit from this year's grants. No one notices they are losing their core managerially or in terms of direction.		
9 Mummies An organisation which can put on its letterheading, 'We were founded in 1751' and is stuck, not able either to die or to change, usually because it is well off and can ignore pressure from users.		
10 Mature adults An organisation or project which is stable, flexible, and responsive. It usually has a high sensitivity to consumer needs, a good managerial framework, a clear vision, and committed and productive staff.		

ACTIVITY 9
STAR CHART: MAPPING RELATIONSHIPS

'I suddenly realised that I had the best relationship with those people who worked in the same building, yet they were the least important for the work I had to do. As a result I started a policy of meeting colleagues from other agencies in town for coffee or lunch several times a week. Working relationships with them have improved significantly since then.'

Aim
to check the quality of individuals' working relationships with key people and organisations, agencies or projects within the network they need to maintain to do their job effectively.

Timing
90 minutes:

40 minutes working individually

20 minutes to display and view each other's star charts

30 minutes for group discussion

Resources needed
large sheet of chart paper and 3 felt tip pens (blue, red, green) for each individual

wall space to display charts, bluetack

facilitator to keep time and lead group discussion

BRIEFING

1 Working individually,

a. list on a separate sheet of paper all the agencies, organisation, projects and/or individuals you have to relate to to get your job done (make sure you do not forget anybody);

b. give each a rating in terms of **their importance to your work**,

(1 (low) to 5 (high));

c give each a rating in terms of **the quality of your working relationship**,

A: relationships with this organisation/person are good

B: relationships are satisfactory but could be improved

C: relationships are unsatisfactory and need urgent attention

2 Draw a small circle in the middle of the chart paper and write your name in the circle.

3 Draw a star to represent each agency, organisation or individual that you have listed on your sheet of paper. Place those agencies or people who are **very important** in your getting your work done close to the centre and those who are **less important** further away from the centre.

If a large agency contains several individuals with whom you work, create a constellation of stars and give each individual their own star.

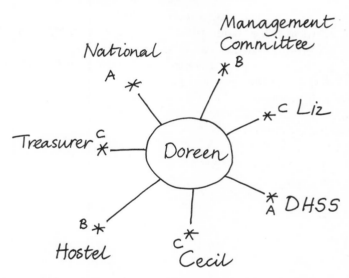

4 Colour each star according to the ratings you have already assigned:

    A – green

    B – blue

    C – red

5 Discuss your chart with a colleague. Look for your patterns among good relationships and among the poor relationships. List any implications that arise for you personally from this exercise.

6 Display charts on a wall and have everyone take the opportunity to look at each other's charts.

7 The facilitator should then draw the team together to discuss any implications that arise from this exercise for the team.

8 Chart these implications, note any necessary action points and agree the next step before closing the session.

ACTIVITY 10
ACTIVE LISTENING

'The first time I was offered an uninterrupted ten minutes to say how I felt, I was sure I could only fill two minutes. Twenty minutes later I was still talking with the ferocity of someone long deprived of genuine attention.'

Aims

to describe three techniques within which individuals or groups can spend time listening to concerns and issues that arise from working together

Timing

variable
working in pairs, 10 minutes +
working in triads, 45 minutes minimum
using the conch, one hour minimum

Resources needed

comfortable, quiet place with few interruptions where individuals can talk confidentially
facilitator to give briefing, keep time, and summarise where appropriate

BRIEFING

1 Boundaries for confidentiality need to be discussed before any of these approaches are used. Individuals should be encouraged not to share any more material with colleagues than they are comfortable with sharing.

2. The facilitator should choose or help the group choose which of the following exercises would be most appropriate in the circumstance:

a Using the conch: this exercise is particularly helpful if at this stage there are serious interersonal blocks in the team.
(i) Use a conch shell or another symbol of some kind, such as a plant or flower;
(ii) the theme will be a phrase given by the facilitator or team members as appropriate. It could be 'why I found it difficult to do these planning exercises' or 'what I feel like working in this team' or 'a time when I felt really very unhappy at work';
(iii) everyone sits in a circle and takes five minutes in turn to speak on the theme, remembering to approach it from their personal feelings or experience, saying 'I......'. The speaker holds the conch shell and no one is allowed to talk except the person holding the shell. The others listen. The person who holds the shell is free to use the five minutes in talking or if not, to sit silently or to pass it on;
(iv) when the facilitator indicates that the five minutes are up, the speaker or the facilitator passes on the shell, trying not to go round in a circle but to take team members at random;
(v) take up to an hour to do this, then take a break. Return and take an hour or so to discuss what has come up, noting in the last 5 or 10 minutes any items that imply future action, and how they will be carried forward.
    You may find it helpful to have an external facilitator but this is also a good and safe exercise to use without one.

b. Working in pairs

(i) select a theme for discussion, e.g. 'how I feel about work', 'things I would like to see different at work';

(ii) select pairs and take 20-30 minutes each to listen to your partner, saying as little as possible and intervening only to clarify or to summarise what you have heard;

(iii) at the end of your joint session, talk briefly about how you felt during this exercise, then make a commitment not to discuss the subject matter during rest of the day (or longer, if that seems appropriate).

c. Working in triads

(i) divide the team into groups of three, who act in turn as
- an observer
- a recipient
- a speaker

(ii) each person when it is their turn as speaker identifies a situation at work with which they are not comfortable; e.g. in which they find it difficult to be assertive, to put their own views clearly, where they feel racial or sexual or other discrimination;

(iii) if the situation seems unclear and muddled, the speaker talks the situation through for an initial set period of approximately 10 minutes, with the person in the role of recipient asking questions to help untangle and clarify their information. At the end of the first period, the observer then adds any comments or observations on what the speaker has been trying to communicate, both with their words and through body language;

(iv) alternatively, if the speaker feels the situation is clear, or if it is a recurring scenario, the speaker may ask instead for help in role-playing the situation, with the aim of examining the speaker's own behaviour, getting suggestions for changes, and rehearsing those suggested changes. The speaker and recipient role-play the situation (with the speaker choosing whether to take his or her own part or to ask the recipient to role-play her initially). The observer helps to analyse and discuss what was happening, remembering that the aim is to help the speaker handle the situation better, not to figure out what the other character 'should' do.

ACTIVITY 11
SETTING A TEAM AGENDA

'Getting issues up front, written up and acknowledged by everybody in the team was a considerable relief after years of grumbling over coffee and behind people's backs.'

Aims

to allow fast, clear sharing and prioritising of tasks, issues and problems in a team or project

Timing

1-2 hours:
10 minutes in pairs
20 minutes in sixes (or fours if a small team)
15 minutes to display cards
30 minutes – 1½ hours for group discussion

Resources needed:

five blank postcards for each individual
A3 or A4 paper or cards, enough for 10 sheets per pair
several tables on which display cards
flipchart or chart paper
facilitator to keep time and lead discussion

———— BRIEFING ————

1 Give all participants 3-5 blank index cards (A4 paper will do) and ask them to break into pairs to discuss issues, concerns, tasks, problems they would like to discuss and work with in the team, on any level, i.e.

Area of concern	e.g.
personal	'I feel under-valued'
practice	'This organisation never involves users in its planning'
policy	'Our equal opportunities policy has never been fully implemented'
organisational	'Junior staff never have a chance to meet the director. Can this be remedied?'
information	'Can someone tell me exactly what our new conditions of service are?

2 Each contribution should be written in clear print, one to a card or sheet of paper. Pairs may have several contributions in one area, none in another. Try not to get lost in generalisations but to give examples with each contribution. Note the general area in which the comment falls, in one corner of the card.

3 Pairs join into groups of four or six to
– share information on the cards;
– identify any common issues;
– write these down together on separate (larger) paper or cards.

It will take a great deal of skill at this point to identify and note common issues without getting so general that they do not mean anything. Again, note one or more examples.

4 Display all cards on tables or on the wall under relevant headings.

5 Have everyone read all the cards, preferably over an extended coffee or tea break. If you have time, it can be helpful to give each participant a felt tip pen or sticky circles and have each person mark the 5 or 10 items they read to which they give the highest priority for attention.

6 The facilitator then
■ charts the main issues arising
■ checks this with participants
■ adds or takes out topics and amalgamates where appropriate

7 Priorities can then be set by simple voting, if necessary. Alternatively, the marks or circles in step 5 can be added up and confirmed.

8 Once the agenda is agreed, the following points also need to be decided:
how, by whom, and when will these issues be dealt with, e.g. in a training session, at a staff meeting, in a memo to the director.

ACTIVITY 12

FACING THE FACTS: EXAMINING THE IMPLICATIONS

'We always felt able to voice our concerns in meetings. It's just that nobody did anything about them.'

Aims

(i) to make sure that ideas, problems, solutions and objectives that arise during planning meetings do not end up just getting lost or shelved;

(ii) to make sure that individuals' feelings about a previous or the present session are heard, understood and if necessary given the time for further expression.

Timing

30 minutes maximum

Resources needed

chart paper and felt tip pens
facilitator to lead discussion and keep time

BRIEFING

1 The facilitator asks each participant to summarise, without interruption or discussion, in under two minutes how they are feeling after the last session.

2 Individuals with strong feelings are invited to make arrangements for doing something about them, e.g. 'I'll talk to Fred over lunch about how confused I am about what he said to me'.

3 The facilitator charts all the issues which have arisen during the session or day that the team feel they will need to do something about. The team should be careful to include issues about their working together, hard as these may be to express clearly.

4 These are prioritised by discussion or voting.

5 Responsibility for the next step for each item is agreed and a target date is set for action to be completed.

6 An individual or individuals agree to circulate the list of what has been agreed and to monitor progress.

ACTIVITY 13
SORTING OUT WHO DOES WHAT

'Booking the room, making the tea and clearing up may not seem as important as saving the world – until nobody does it!'

Aim
to help teams allocate work clearly, fairly and openly

Timing
variable

Resources needed
flip chart or chart paper
facilitator to keep time and lead discussion

———— BRIEFING ————

1 List all the activities or tasks that need doing in priority order, if necessary by voting.

2 Ask for volunteers to take on the work and list their names on the chart next to the task they have chosen.

3 Allocate work still outstanding. List names on chart.

4 Ask each person to take 10 minutes to check whether they still can/want to/should take on the task or tasks, bearing in mind their existing workload. (You may find it helpful to refer back to the information you noted from **Activity 3 Your Working Week.**) The facilitator makes it clear that if the person still decides to take on the task, he needs to set a reasonable deadline.

5 If you wish, you may try to trade or off-load current work if this is the only way you can take on new work.

6 The facilitator reconvenes the group to:
– examine the implications of what individuals have decided about who can or will do what;
– if necessary, drop items of work for which no one is willing or able to accept responsibility;
– renegotiate work that for statutory reasons must be done, even if no one wants to do it – or formulate a memo for senior officers if every member of the team feels they have no scope to take on additional work without senior help in setting priorities;
– add places, dates and names to the list;
– get agreement about who will type, circulate and agree to monitor the progress of the various tasks.

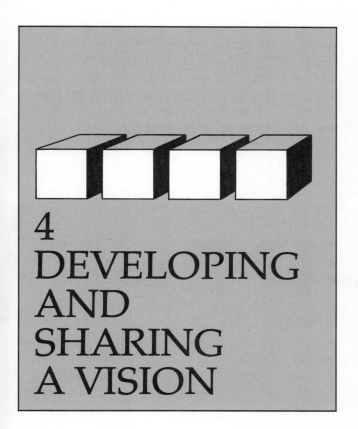

4
DEVELOPING AND SHARING A VISION

If you are going to get anywhere together, you need to agree where you are going, sharing a vision of what success or action you seek.

The first talk about holidays over coffee at work in midwinter revealed a variety of dreams. Jane's idea of a break was a walking tour in the Pennines with the ramblers' club. Floyd and his wife preferred visiting members of their church choir network in Birmingham, and were saving up to have a long holiday in Trinidad sometime in the future: George, Sue, Eric and Bhavna all complained of having missed sunshine last year and were desperate to have a good sunny holiday this year.

But when the sea was mentioned, Eric quickly counted himself out. He hated the ocean and had visions of a river or lake in France or Germany, when everyone else was dreaming of palm trees and ocean waves. So it was Sue, David and Bhavna who initially met with other friends and partners and talked about holidays in the sun near a beach.

Knowing that you share a vision of where you are going in your work, however large or small your organisation, is the foundation of planning and the reference point for review and evaluation. For small organisations this is important because so much of the history and continuity is carried by a few workers.

'Half our workers are new this year, and all of a sudden we have lost our tradition of campaigning for the homeless. And several workers and residents have commented on a shift of emphasis in our work with residents. As one of the residents said to me recently.

''When I first moved into these houses it was for single homeless people and for some reason it's slowly turning into a mental ward''.'

If you are part of a small team within a large organisation or local authority, it is equally important that you know how your own individual and team vision fits within the vision of the larger organisation. You can assume your common purpose is self-evident, e.g. to provide housing benefits to all those eligible in the borough; to get aircraft off the ground; to give out supplementary benefits. Yet even within these broad frames of reference, the visions can differ widely. Take the example of housing benefits sections within two different local authorities. Both have the same initial statement of purpose, 'We aim to provide housing benefits to those people who are entitled to them'. But for one this means,

'We have to keep the rules. But, within those rules, we want to make sure that people get as much as they can.'

For the other,

'Our task is to give out housing benefits to those who ask, not to do community work to encourage those who do not enquire.'

If each of you in your team asked the question, 'what are we here for?' or 'where do we want to go together?' do you think your answers would have a lot in common?

The whole planning process depends on your being able to answer these questions as a team. From your shared vision comes your ability to decide how you are going to work together to put it into practice. Even a shared sense of where you differ will alert you to some of the difficulties you may face.

A team without a shared, and stated, purpose is like a bicycle wheel without a hub. Instead of each aim and objective being connected to the central vision, a lot of activities, and individuals, will be flying around with little to show for it.

Without a shared vision, how do you know how to

■ deal with conflicting demands both from within your organisation and from outside it?

■ evaluate on your own terms as a team?

■ set priorities for the work of each individual, or write a job description?

Yet many of us are tempted to pass over this stage. Sometimes this is because we assume we know what we are doing together. At other times it is because we assume we will not agree and therefore do not want to open the can of worms. Either assumption may be incorrect.

For example, a group of women running a women's centre collectively had assumed that they all agreed on what they are doing and why. When a consultant was called in to help them with what they thought were terrible personality conflicts, she discovered that in fact they had no shared sense of their purpose or direction.

Developing a vision is not an exact science. It is a matter of getting a statement of purpose right sufficiently for you as a team to feel comfortable in working towards it for the time being.

Two examples of more complex statements of vision are illustrated below. The first is from a joint health authority and social services community alcohol team. The second is from the human resources (personnel) department in a large organisation. Further illustrations are included in the activities at the end of this chapter.

Health Service/Social Services Community Alcohol Team
THE FUTURE SERVICE

The CAT team is committed to the development and extension of existing services. Future services will take account of the need to develop training and consultancy services in line with the original CAT philosophy.

Accordingly the team has agreed the following CORE VISION:

AIMS (why)
To reduce the cost to the community of alcohol misuse
i.e. lost hours of work
    marital breakdown
    abuse of children
    conflict with the law
    related medical costs

OBJECTIVES (what)
To improve the quality of life of the individuals and/or the families and friends who have problems with or related to alcohol use/misuse.

SERVICES (how)
The team will attempt to provide the following services:
These services are listed in priority order.
1. Assesment support counselling and information about safe drinking for individuals, friends, carers.
2. Education and training to other professionals and support services to other professionals i.e. doctor social workers, probation officers, teachers, nurses, police, personnel officers.
3. Other educational activity – in particular aimed at the general public.

(who)
The service will be provided by a closely-knit trained co-ordinated multi-disciplinary team who are ea accessible to the public and other professionals 9–5 p.m. 5 days a week.

AND
regularly to evaluate the effectiveness of the service.

Human Resources (Personnel) Department
MISSION STATEMENT

To support managers in the achievement of their business goals through realising the full potential of their people.

To develop managers and their teams so their full resources are available to meet business objectives.

To be seen by managers as the prime source of advice and counsel.

To develop systems to support and sustain the management of initiatives.

To be an integrated part of the department seen by all as a reliable, accurate source of support and information.

To lead in identifying, proposing and exploring ideas through which the organisation may develop and change to meet its customer needs.

To be enjoyable and fulfilling team in which to work, providing opportunities to learn and promoting the desire for self-improvement.

To reflect professional excellence through our own team development and example.

You may have noticed that we have used the words 'vision' and 'purpose' interchangeably. There are many other words used to describe this stage, such as 'mission statement', 'aims', 'goals', 'core mission'. We have chosen 'vision' or 'purpose' because these seem most closely to meet the needs of many workers to remind them of the meaning of what they are doing. Choose the phrase which seems to suit you as a team.

────────ACTIVITIES────────

The main point of creating a statement of vision or purpose is that you develop it together. You may prefer to have a simple statement of your central vision, such as

'We are here to improve the quality of life of the frail elderly and relatives who care for them.'

Activity 14: Creating a Statement of Purpose introduces a way of coming to such an agreed single statement, building on each worker's vision.

Activity 15: Drawing a Vision helps you to debate what your project exists for and to test whether you can communicate this visually.

Some teams find it more helpful to express their purpose in a way that states who they are working with, where they are operating, why they are doing what they are doing, and how they will work, as a team and with users. **Activity 16: Agreeing a Vision** introduces a process that breaks the statement down in that way.

──DEALING WITH COMMON── ──────PITFALLS──────

Achieving a good statement of purpose is one of the most rewarding experiences a team can go through. It generally builds a great deal of cohesion and commitment. But it can take a long while to get there and be both emotionally and physically draining en route.

Convincing the sceptics

It may be difficult to convince some members of the team that this is worth doing, especially if they are part of a large bureaucracy and feel they are there simply to get on with the job. The commitment of the team leader is the crucial factor.

In the year we first tried to make a statement of our purpose. I almost could not go through with it, as team leader, because of a conflict with a member of my team. He was not only doodling ostentatiously throughout the sessions, he at one point reached over and rifled through the papers on my chair. Finally I got the courage to say to him, "Look, I am doing what I feel is necessary for our team at this point. I am asking you to trust that enough to see it through, then at the end of the day if you still feel it was useless, say so". I could hardly get the sentences out, I was so choked up, but finally we made it. And during the year that ground-work saw us through a loss of staff, crises with young people, dealing with the absence and severe depression of another member of our team. Making sense of what we were up to had also helped us to share the crises en route. I was amazed at the security that that initial work gave us all.

Taking care of yourselves

Do not add any extra stress to that which the process itself creates. Work in a space that is friendly and comfortable. Take time for good breaks. Eat well.

Getting stuck

At some point in the process, people often experience a point of confusion and blackness, where the whole thing feels hopeles, and/or pointless. This is the point where people start getting tired and irritable. Some may say, 'we're giving too much time to these words' and be tempted to let words or phrases go into the statement with which they are not really comfortable.

This is a tricky stage for the facilitator who needs to be sensitive to the need for breaks while reminding the team that perseverance will pay off. (The first time you do this, you will simply have to trust us that the process works; after that, you can speak from your own experience.)

Getting stuck on words may signal being stuck in working together, so working through the verbal blockage may alter other ways in which the team operates.

Keeping it public

Everyone needs to see what is going on at each step, otherwise the process of building up the statement and refining it gets lost. For this you will need large sheets of paper or a large blackboard and space on the walls to spread out sheets as they accumulate.

Dealing with conflict

The attempt to create a joint statement may throw up conflicts about the purpose of your work. If compromise does not seem possible, you have a serious problem. It may be useful to bring in an outside consultant at this point, or, if you are working with one, to stop and deal with the conflicts directly. Ignoring the differences will not make them go away. They will simply surface again when you are under the most stress.

Losing individuals

The history of the organisation of which the team is a part will be a combination of written statements from employers and organisational and community mythology, much of it oral history. The task of sharing a vision is to take all this received information into account, and in addition, include the visions of each new member of the team. Listening carefully to each individual is crucial if everyone is to have a stake in the outcome. When you are creating the statement, if one person is unhappy with a single word, then time needs to be taken to work that through.

Avoiding platitudes

Your statement of purpose should be a working tool, not just platitudes for an annual report. It will be the basis on which more concrete aims, objectives and activities will be based. Try to develop sensitivity both as participants and facilitator for language that gets too woolly. A broad vision can be stated clearly without being a platitude. For example,

We aim to promote more and better play opportunities for all children, especially in disadvantaged areas.

rather than,

We aim to encourage children to play

Testing it

Often a good test of the statement is to ask whether a stranger or member of the public could understand fairly accurately what you are trying to say. Could your users understand it? This, after all, is about work for and with them.

The final test is to sleep on it. Arrange at a meeting a few days later to check that everyone is still happy with the statement before moving on to translate it into aims, objectives and action plans.

ACTIVITY 14
CREATING A STATEMENT OF PURPOSE

'We tried this exercise at our AGM. It was a shock to realise how many diverse and different views there were about why the organisation existed. No wonder we seemed to be in the midst of constant disagreement about policy.'

Aim
to help a team create a single statement that clarifies its reason for being.

Timing
2-3 hours:
15 minutes working individually
1½-2½ hours in the group

Resources needed
chart paper, pens
facilitator to keep time and lead discussion

—————— BRIEFING ——————

1 Each person takes 15-20 minutes to write down one to two sentences that in their view describes the reason for the team's existence, e.g.
'helping elderly people lead a better life';
'reducing accidents among elderly residents';
'encouraging the community to care better for old people'.

2 The facilitator then lists these on a chart and encourages team members to look at areas of agreement, e.g.
'we all agree we work with the elderly (but do we call them senior citizens, old people, elderly, or over 65s?)'
and areas of disagreement, e.g.
'are we going to help directly or do we want to encourage the community to help?'

3 The facilitator helps the team continue to amalgamate and refine the sentences, with the eventual aim of creating a single statement with which everyone can agree, e.g.
'we aim to improve the quality of life of frail elderly people and relatives who care for them by offering support to carers'.

4 The facilitator encourages the team to pause for several days before they move on to the next stage in planning, and arranges a time for them to meet and consider whether the statement they agreed still seems acceptable and appropriate to each of them.

ACTIVITY 15
DRAWING A VISION

'We all knew why we existed as a project, yet explaining it to others in the simple language of a poster was more difficult than we could possibly have imagined.'

Aims

(i) to help a team simplify its vision so that it could be easily communicated to users and to the general public;
(ii) to give team members an opportunity to work together in articulating this vision.

Timing

2-3 hours

Resources needed

large amounts of chart paper, coloured pens, paints, newsprint, old magazines, scissors, paste, bluetack
a facilitator to keep time and lead discussion

——— BRIEFING ———

1 The team breaks into groups of between four and six, each group imagining that it is an advertising agency charged with the task of designing a poster that can
a. sell the project, piece of work or organisation to users;
b. describe reasonably accurately and truthfully what the project or organisation does;
c. be attractive and easy to read.

2 Each team member works for 20-30 minutes on their own to produce several rough sketches, e.g.

3 The facilitator draws the groups together to seek to final agreement on a design with which everyone is happy.

Remember that the purpose of the exercise is to help you debate what your project exists for and to test whether it can be communicated simply. The best posters are produced by teams who work well together.

4 If several teams or syndicates have taken part, these posters can be displayed and discussed in a large group setting. Individual groups may wish to present their posters to the entire group, giving reasons for its design.

Particular attention needs to be paid to how similar the overall message is in each of the posters.

Is there full agreement as to the nature of the organisation's work or are there real practical and philosophical difference emerging? If so, these may need to be noted and discussed.

A vote may be taken on the poster that is deemed best to represent the work of the team.

5 The facilitator may also wish to get the team members to comment on how well, or not, they managed to work together, and to note any implications this might have for future working.

ACTIVITY 16
AGREEING A VISION

'Talking together about why we were there, sharing differences of opinion, compromising on our less important issues was hard work but eventually made us feel part of a team that mattered and knew where it was going.'

Aims
(i) to help the team produce a clearly written statement of vision as a basis for all future work;
(ii) to produce a framework within which differences of opinion and approach can be addressed;
(iii) to create a basis for a group of individuals to have the sense of being a team.

Timing
3-6 hours, depending on
a. membership of team
b. levels of familiarity and trust amongst team members
c. levels of disagreement around key issues.

Resources needed
Comfortable room with wall space for display
chart paper and bluetack
experienced facilitator to lead discussion and chart results

BRIEFING
---

1 Break into groups of three or four individuals, or in small teams, working individually for 30 minutes to one hour. Try to produce a written poster (with no pictures) which represents the individual's or group's vision of why the organisation, team or project exists. Portray this under five headings:
a. who are we working with?
    who are our clients/customers/patients/users?
b. where do we work, e.g. the village, town, city, county, country, universe?
c. why are we doing this work, i.e. what are we trying to achieve?
d. how do we propose to do this, i.e. working methods, campaigning, giving away blankets, educating, training?
Also make as optional the following category:
a. things the group or the individual may think are important, such as working collectively, not being paid, users managing the service.

2 All these posters are then displayed together. While everyone else is having a coffee break, the facilitator tries to amalgamate the statements under each heading, showing areas of agreement and areas of disagreement.

Where

Group 1	Group 2
The local village	The county
Group 3	Group 4
The country	The world

A discussion clearly needs to take place to decide the boundaries for the team's work. Similarly,

Who

Group 1	Group 2
Elderly people	Frail elderly people
Group 3	Group 4
Disabled elderly people	Unemployed young people

3 The facilitator then leads the group through each issue until agreement is reached. Great emphasis should be placed on
a. what words actually mean
b. listening for disagreements
c. encouraging proper debate
d. valuing everyone's contribution
e. statements being clear and understandable.

4 Eventually a group statement is written up with which everyone feels they can agree, for example

STATEMENT for a social work team

WHO

We aim to help individuals who have mental health problems which are leading them to fail to cope with essential life routines. These problems should neither place them or their dependants at high risk of protracted institutional care, physical injury or permanent emotional damage. We would also work with individuals whose level of functioning requires a high degree of care, protection or supervision.

WHERE/WHY

We would generally only work with individuals who live within the Health District referred by other professionals or voluntary agencies. We broadly aim to improve the quality of life of those individuals and families with whom we come into contact by enabling them to improve functioning, self-image and potential, representing their needs to others or by offering legal protection.

HOW

By providing access to skilled person-centred helpers who can work with individuals to help them assess their problems, and enable them to set clear, manageable goals. This should take place within multidisciplinary teams. Individuals should have access to a wide range or services including practical help, rehabilitation, family and marital work, individual and group counselling, advocacy, statutory work and referral to other agencies.

QUALITY

We would seek to do this within the climate that encourages maximum client participation, effective team support and manageable workloads. We would seek to encourage the development of primary care services, particularly for those individuals who fall outside our team priorities, but who clearly need access to appropriate help.

In order to arrive at this statement the following are some of the debates we had to have:

helping people by giving them advice
vs
offering them treatment

---

working alone as a team
vs
working with other professionals

---

providing varieties of kinds of help
vs
providing only one kind of help

---

only working with people who are at very high risk of injury and in institutional care already
vs
concentrating on preventing people getting ill

---

being an agency that accepts its statutory responsibilities
vs
whether these should be passed on to others

---

making service available to anyone who walks in the door
vs
limited to referral from other professionals

---

using trained staff
vs
using volunteers

---

5 Take time to comment on the process of working together, asking
- how are people feeling?
- are they happy with the statement?
- does each person feel they have had the opportunity to make the contribution they wanted to?

6 Leave at least 24 hours before meeting again to check whether the statement is still acceptable to each member of the team.

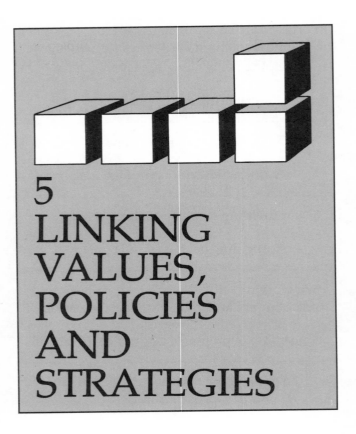

5
LINKING VALUES, POLICIES AND STRATEGIES

The statement of purpose is only a statement of intent. The next step is deciding on the range of ways you are going to carry it out and what you find acceptable and unacceptable behaviour en route, both individually and as a team.

The group of friends shared a vision, a holiday on a beach in the sun. They had to learn that members of the group had different ideas about how to put this into practice.

'On holiday it was sometimes hard to keep harmony. We realised that we had different values and beliefs about all sorts of things including children being seen and heard, bedtimes, diet and privacy. We had discussed all this after the camping weekend and had agreed that whatever the complaints, each family had to sort things out their own way, unless the complaint involved all of us, and then we needed to raise it, not just have some of the group bottle it up or go off in a sulk.'

The stage of looking at personal values, establishing policies and agreeing strategies is often missed out or muddled in planning together, at great risk to the chances of success for your work.

As an example, a centre has been adapted to provide access and facilities for those with disabilities. Everyone agreed to this. Now that it is available, what seem to be two different camps have emerged. Those whose values are based on self-determination and self-help for those with disabilities want a policy of hiring the centre only to groups with a direct involvement in disability

issues. Others whose values are about integrating those with disabilities and those who are able-bodied in more general contexts, want a policy of hiring the facilities out to any groups who wish to broaden the participation of people with disabilities, whether they are involved with disability or not.

The unravelling of purpose, value, policies and strategies looks a bit like this:

VISION OR PURPOSE
an overall statement of what you are doing together

VALUES
your personal vision of the way you see the world and what you believe about people

SHARED VALUES
the values which underpin your work together and your relationships with your users

STRATEGIES
the path, means or method of converting your vision into action

POLICIES
statement of intent about the quality of the work you are undertaking and a formal expression of the culture of the organisation

AIMS
what you want and need to do

The following is an example of how this stage was expressed in a local authority housing benefits department.

```
┌─────────────────────────────────────┐
│              VISION                  │
│  We aim to provide housing benefits  │
│  to those people who are entitled    │
│  to them                             │
└─────────────────────────────────────┘
                  │
┌─────────────────────────────────────┐
│          SHARED VALUES               │
│  We have to obey the rules but       │
│  within those rules we want to make  │
│  sure people get as much as they can │
└─────────────────────────────────────┘

┌──────────────────┐  ┌──────────────────┐
│    POLICIES      │  │    STRATEGIES    │
│  find ways to    │  │  urging people   │
│  help those who  │  │  to claim        │
│  find it hard to │  │  benefits        │
│  contact us      │  │                  │
│                  │  │  telling people  │
│  treat everyone  │  │  about other     │
│  fairly          │  │  benefits they   │
│                  │  │  can get and     │
│                  │  │  helping them    │
│                  │  │  claim           │
└──────────────────┘  └──────────────────┘

┌─────────────────────────────────────┐
│              AIMS                    │
│  running a postal advertising        │
│  campaign in the borough urging      │
│  those eligible to claim             │
│                                      │
│  circulating a special               │
│  questionnaire to all                │
│  those with disabilities,            │
│  using disability                    │
│  organisations, social               │
│  services, and our own               │
│  records                             │
│                                      │
│  making staff time                   │
│  available to follow                 │
│  through on the results              │
│  of the questionnaire                │
└─────────────────────────────────────┘
```

The human resources (personnel) department whose core vision is given as an example in the previous chapter also worked out their philosophy and values and presented them in this way:

Philosophy and Values

■ work from the basis that everyone has something to contribute

■ work *with* other people as much as possible to create commitment and ownership

■ within the department there will be collective responsibility for leadership and decisions

■ our politics will be positive, designed to benefit the larger departmental and organisational goals rather than self interest

■ we will be a breeding ground for knowledge, skills and values that the company espouses and uses

■ we will use all the resources open to us, inside and outside the organisation, for maximum and positive impact

■ we will be constantly looking to identify our learnings and improve ourselves through all the things we do, both good and bad.

Although we have presented this information in a diagrammatic format, in fact the relationship between values, policy and strategies is much more dynamic. Demands may come from users that challenge your policies and strategies. For example, many catering sections of schools, colleges, hospitals and local authorities have in recent years been under pressure to provide food that reflects ethnic preferences as well as those of vegetarians. This demand may not have affected the purpose of the departments, to feed their workforce or patients or students nutritionally and economically, but it may have raised issues of policy and strategy that most catering managers had not considered 10 years ago.

ACTIVITIES

Each of the activities in this section is designed to help you unpick the issues of values, policies and strategies and how these relate to your behaviour at work.

Activity 17: Looking at Differences in Commitment will enable each person in the team to place themselves and everyone else in relation to a value they hold important to the team's work. This is done as a aid to discussion.

Activity 18: Identifying Clashes between Intentions and Behaviour should help members of a team to face areas where their intentions and behaviour are not in accord, without assigning 'fault' and 'blame'.

Activity 19: How Far Will I Go? offers you a checklist to test what your limits are in implementing a particular policy or belief.

Activity 20: Sharing Values should help the team negotiate the values which all members agree should inform their work as a team.

──DEALING WITH COMMON── ──PITFALLS──

Even discussing issues in this area is a minefield, as it touches us in areas of deepest purpose and commitment on the one hand and in our sense of what it is like to be a member of society on the other.

Tablets of stone
Few of us share the same beliefs, if not the same values, in the same way and with the same intensity throughout our lives, and that will be true for your team as well. Recognise that you simply need at intervals to stand back and reflect on how you are working together. It should not be seen as a loss of face to alter any of these factors.

'We had gone on ad nauseum about collective working then one day, for us, we faced the fact that it did not work and went about trying to restructure things to keep the same principles, about involving everyone, while having a senior worker. It took us ages because we felt somehow that we had let the side down.'

Respecting boundaries
However we work together, we remain individuals with private lives as well. It is important to differentiate between values we might hold generally and our behaviour at work. For example, in your heart of hearts you may not believe that women should be playing the role they are in management. That is, in fact, your business. What is important, if you are in a team the bases its work on a policy of equal opportunities and dealing with oppression, is how you actually treat any woman in a management position. That is the business of the team.

Checking out
It is important to keep checking at each stage of planning how it relates to your own values and to your stated policies as a team. Many teams are finding, under pressure, that they are seduced away from their policies by the prospect of money or expansion. It is not wrong to change direction; it is simply healthier for your work as a team and your communication with users if you are doing this consciously and explicitly.

ACTIVITY 17
LOOKING AT DIFFERENCES IN COMMITMENT

'Having come from a team where my beliefs and values were constantly under threat and where I felt personally alienated, I'm thankful to be with a group of colleagues who seem to share my values. Also, they support me both personally and practically when these values are put to the test.'

Aims

(i) to help working teams face and understand the implications of individual differences in commitment to identified values;
(ii) to provide a forum where these differences can be shared and explored in a constructive manner;
(iii) to clarify areas of agreement and disagreement about values and beliefs.

Timing

1½ hours:
20 minutes working individually
80 minutes working in the group

Resources needed

A4 sheets of paper listing all participants names, photocopied so that each person has a sheet;
a facilitator to keep time and lead discussion

——— BRIEFING ———

1 The team or facilitator needs to select a value or belief that is relevant to the team's work, e.g. 'users should have open access to all written material held by the team about them.'

2 The facilitator leads a discussion for approximately 30 minutes, during which time the meaning of the statement can be debated and clarified.

3 Each individual then spends 20 minutes on their own rating **their opinion** of the commitment of each team member to this principle, on the following scale:

+5   **actively committed**
+4
+3
+2
+1
 0   **neutral**
−1
−2
−3
−4
−5   **actively against**

4 These forms are handed in anonymously. The team members take a tea break while the group leader collates the scores against the name of each individual, on a flip chart, e.g.

John   4   3   3   2   2
Marcus −1 −2 −1 −1 −1
Renu   5   4   5   5   4

5 The group is invited to discuss the implications of these scores, each individual having a chance to comment on their own scores first.

6 The issue is then debated again and any implications for the work of the agency are noted.

7 Anything needing action is recorded and someone takes responsibility for the next step.

ACTIVITY 18

IDENTIFYING CLASHES BETWEEN INTENTIONS AND BEHAVIOUR

'For the past several years we have talked endlessly about the need for the team to reflect the composition of the neighbourhood it serves. By far the majority of residents now are black and Asian. Yet we are still a white middle-class team, and most of us are male.'

Aim

to help teams identify areas where intentions and behaviour are not in accord

Timing

1 hour:
working individually 15 minutes
viewing cards   15 minutes
discussion   15 minutes

Resources needed

100 blank postcards
flip chart or chart paper
a facilitator to keep time and lead group discussion

BRIEFING

1 Individuals are asked to spend about 15 minutes writing down, anonymously if they wish, examples where identified values held by the individual, the team, and/or the organisation are contradicted by the behaviour of the individual, the team, the organisation, e.g.

personal
'I still often expect secretaries to make tea and wash up, even though intellectually I feel it is wrong.'

team
'We talk about being a collective but decisions still seem to get made by a few people.'

organisation
'We talk about being committed to equal opportunities for people with disabilities but still have done nothing about wheelchair access.'

2 All the cards are displayed on a table and everyone has the opportunity to read them.

3 The facilitator leads a group discussion and attempts to summarise on chart paper the main issues which have arisen.

4 Each issue is then debated and agreement reached on
a. what needs to be done;
b. who will do it; and
c. by when it will be done.

ACTIVITY 19
HOW FAR WILL I GO?

'Looking at the television news of civil disturbances in this country and around the world, I wondered at what point my own beliefs and principles might come into conflict with friends, colleagues, or the law. I am not clear how far I would be prepared to go to defend my own beliefs.'

Aim

to help individuals and then teams to explore how far they would be prepared to go in defence of certain principles.

Timing

1½ hours

15 minutes working individually

30 minutes in pairs

45 minutes in group discussions

Resources needed

copy of *How Far Will I Go?* questionnaire for each person

facilitator to keep time and lead discussion

BRIEFING

1 Each individual spends 15 minutes reading the checklist and making notes about the circumstances in which they would be prepared to behave in the way listed, e.g.

Confronting colleagues' bad behaviour

'I'm willing if necessary to challenge the use of violence by colleagues on children in school.'

2 Each person then spends 30 minutes with a colleague in confidential discussion, exploring the answers each has given.

3 The facilitator, and/or team, picks a topic relevant to the team for group discussion, e.g. racist behaviour, and invites participants to discuss how far the team is willing to challenge racist behaviour within the team or organisation.

The checklist may be used again if discussion flags.

4 The facilitator attempts to gain agreement as to the limits the team will put on tackling racist behaviour, e.g. *'Points 1-11 on the checklist agreed; breaking the law is not agreed.'*

The team may wish to continue this discussion about other areas where they face such decisions in their work together.

5 The facilitator checks out how individuals are feeling.

6 Any further discussion and work that needs to be done by the team or between individual members is noted and a time and place agreed.

HOW FAR WILL I GO?
CHECKLIST

Where would you draw the line in putting beliefs and principles into practice? Note beside each item the circumstances in which you feel you would take such action.

1 Disturbing comfortable working routines.

2 Doing things that made me uncomfortable.

3 Confronting a colleague's bad behaviour.

4 Talking about my views and beliefs in the staff room.

5 Confronting colleagues in a formal meeting.

6 Refusing to carry out certain menial but meaningful activities on principle.

7 Talking to a potentially hostile public meeting about where I stand.

8 Risking the disapproval of my peers.

9 Risking getting emotionally upset in defence of my beliefs and values.

10 Turning down a promotion if it meant having to take on principles and behaviour contrary to my own.

11 Resigning rather than compromising my beliefs.

12 Breaking byelaws I did not think were just.

13 Refusing to pay rates or taxes.

14 Committing criminal acts if I felt they were justified in relation to my cause.

15 Going to prison for my principles.

ACTIVITY 20
SHARING VALUES

'It took me a long time to understand that collective working for this team was not just a statement in the job descriptions but a way of life. Gradually I realised I could not go that far and left.'

Aim

to help the team articulate and agree on the values by which they are committed to working

Timing

2-3 hours

Resources needed

flip chart or blackboard, chart paper, felt pens

3 postcards per person

comfortable conference room with *no interruptions* and coffee and tea available

one person allocated as facilitator to guide discussion, arbitrate, and help the team face potential conflicts of value.

———— BRIEFING ————

1 The facilitator introduces the session by outlining the importance of articulating values. She or he reminds people that many of the issues may be emotive, that it will be particularly important for everyone to listen carefully to each other and to give feedback assertively rather than destructively.

2 Each person spends 15 minutes on their own thinking about and writing down on a postcard up to three values or principles they consider should govern the work of the team, e.g.

a. as workers we should be on time for meetings and appointments, as a mark of respect to others with whom we work

b. the organisation should seek to maximise the participation of users both in the day-to-day running of projects and in policy making

c. staff with dependent children should be given every facility both to work effectively and to meet their obligations as parents

3 Display the cards on a table and give everyone the opportunity to read them.

4 Team members should divide into small groups, if the team is larger than five, and each group decide on their priority values. This may require group members to negotiate and amalgamate their individual contributions.

5 In the full group the facilitator needs to chart the priority lists from each group. In discussion, the aim is for the team to reach agreement about the three values which they feel are most important to be committed to in their work as a team.

6 Agree any action necessary, who will do it and by when.

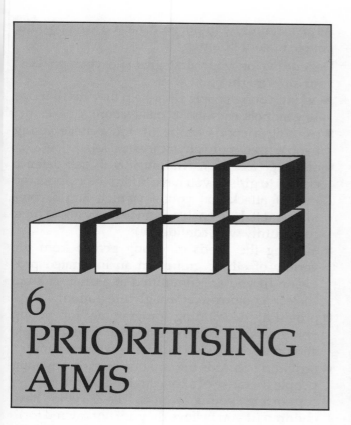

6
PRIORITISING AIMS

Once you have agreed where you are going and how you need to get there, it is time to identify what you want and need to do.

The group of friends planning the holiday discovered there was a lot more to it than sun and beach. Work had been tiring for everyone and they wanted to break to get recharged. They wanted a situation where they could be with friends, when they felt like it, or could go off on their own. Jean was sure her teenagers would want access to a disco, but neither she nor any of the other adults wanted a camp site where there was a noisy disco every night. No one felt affluent, so economy was an important consideration. The women made it clear that their idea of a holiday was not cooking and cleaning (two of the men pointed out that it was not their idea of a holiday either). Several keen sailors wanted the group to pool funds and hire a sailboat for the week.

This group of friends had begun the process of crystallising their vision and clarifying the direction it would take. As you can see, the direction was influenced not only by their purpose but by their values, e.g. they wanted to meet the needs of the children by having them near a disco but without jeopardising the priority for the adults of having a quiet, recharging holiday.

When all the the aims were on the table, as Jean pointed out, 'We found we had a hard time setting priorities. Those of is who really felt broke preferred to forego the boat, as did those who simply wanted to be on the beach. We adults decided that if we couldn't have both the disco and the quiet, we'd do without access to a disco in favour of a quiet site.'

What would have happened had they skipped this stage and gone straight into making arrangements? Were they just wasting time and energy? This stage is a bridge between the scope of vision and the preciseness about what individuals need to do to further it. It is the stage of getting clearer about your direction without getting sidetracked into too much detail. If you miss it out, you endanger the development of a sense of coherence to your team's work and the opportunity of relating each individual's work to the whole.

Getting more specific is a three-step process. The first stage is to identify and prioritise aims that reflect your purpose. Then for each of the aims you will need to set objectives and draw up action plans. For a team working with the frail elderly, the process looked like this:

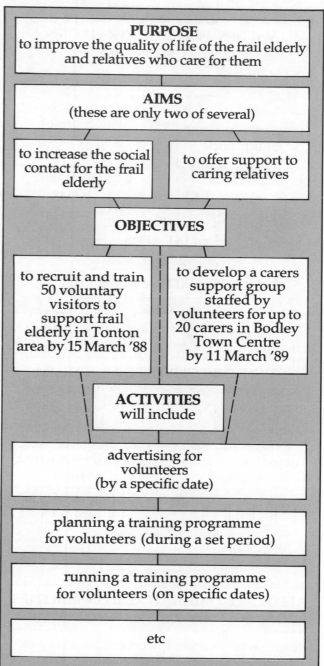

PURPOSE
to improve the quality of life of the frail elderly and relatives who care for them

AIMS
(these are only two of several)

| to increase the social contact for the frail elderly | to offer support to caring relatives |

OBJECTIVES

| to recruit and train 50 voluntary visitors to support frail elderly in Tonton area by 15 March '88 | to develop a carers support group staffed by volunteers for up to 20 carers in Bodley Town Centre by 11 March '89 |

ACTIVITIES
will include

advertising for volunteers
(by a specific date)

planning a training programme for volunteers (during a set period)

running a training programme for volunteers (on specific dates)

etc

It is helpful to develop the ability to move between these stages, to be able to look at an activity and know how it relates to your aim and vision, or to see in an aim the implications of the detailed objectives and activities. This will enable each worker to place her or his own work in perspective. An awareness of the different stages may point to the direction other work may take, e.g. aiming to train volunteers may require that members of staff themselves get support to develop training skills. It is at this stage of identifying aims that the work in the previous chapters on values, policy and strategies need to be incorporated, in the following way:

As an example, your purpose may be to help young people in your borough.

Depending on your strategies and your policies, your aims might be:

- asking young people what help they need (if one of your policies is about consultation);
- running a sports centre (if you believe young people need more physical exercise);
- offering assertion training and self-defence classes to girls (if you have information about the rate of attacks on young women and a commitment to help enable them to move about their community with confidence);
- meeting the needs of young people from the variety of ethnic groups in an integrated provision (if you are committed to a multi-cultural society as expressed through integration);
- providing a training programme for young volunteers (if you believe that young people should be enabled to run their own provision);
- providing an Aids information service for young people (because of a concern for health);
- supporting young women 14-21 who have children (if you believe they are not catered for).

None of these aims are right or wrong. They follow on from different commitments, policies and strategies.

Your vision of 'helping young people in your borough' may have generated 15 aims. You will need to decide which of these are your priorities, as you are unlikely to have time for all of them, and certainly not for all of them at once. Research into time management reinforces this point: not only will you not have the time, but you simply cannot keep track of more than seven to nine priorities at once.

We are looking here at one aim at a time. Of course no piece of work stands in isolation from the rest of the work of the team and from how you are managing to work together. At this stage you will need to take into account not only the aims generated for this particular area of work but ones that were generated when you are taking stock and any that arose when you were developing values, policies and strategies.

ACTIVITIES

Activity 21: Negotiating Priorities allows a team to identify and prioritise aims within a method of negotiation.

If prioritising aims has thrown up any conflicts or contradictions, you may want to return to **Activity 12: Facing the Facts: Dealing with the Implications** to help look at what has been done and decide what you are going to do about the outcomes.

DEALING WITH COMMON PITFALLS

Reality checks

The work in time management indicates that we cannot deal effectively with more than seven to nine major areas of interest in our lives. It is worth keeping this in mind when aims become too hard to prioritise and you feel like letting that one 'just slip in' for now. Some day someone is going to have to do something with it. The further down the road you get with aims which you already know, or sense, you cannot meet, the harder it is to drop them and the more time and energy you have wasted.

The danger of override

Priorities are not simply logical pursuits of our vision; they are directions in which we want to go that are often influenced by deeply-held beliefs, by ambition, by fear. It is important in a team that these individual commitments and drives are recognised and incorporated. This should enrich the work of the team rather than divert it from its stated purpose. For this reason, it is important to keep referring back to the statement of purpose the team has developed together. Ask yourselves, 'How far does this priority meet our vision? How far have we drifted away?' If there is a drift and everyone feels OK about it, it may be necessary to go back and alter the team statement of vision. It is not wrong to change your course. Doing so by default will leave the team open to gaps that will make monitoring, evaluation and the shared development of the work more difficult.

Prioritising priorities

Many teams in voluntary and statutory services, as well as in business, are facing the tension between a decrease in resources and a growth in demand for their services.

One social services team leader said, 'We are no longer simply setting priorities. We have already done that. Now we are having to set priorities within priorities. For instance, do we choose to put the bulk of our resources into work with children at risk or work with the elderly? Our choice may mean choosing who is left to die first. In the present climate, we know we have to choose the work with children.'

This is a reality for many teams. No matter what the constraints, clarity about aims and priorities will give the team a rationale by which to communicate its discussions and actions both to users and to managers. It will also allow individual workers to manage their own workloads.

Compulsory priorities

Teams in certain kinds of work have aims set for them by law; others have them set by the company. This does not make the stage of identifying and setting priorities irrelevant. Feedback from many organisations and from across the country indicates that within these compulsory aims there may be options of approach. These may range from the choice of working with individuals or groups; of working in neighbourhoods rather than centrally; of integrating services with other sectors rather than working in isolation. This feedback also indicates that for worker satisfaction and service effectiveness, workers need aims that recognise their needs for support and satisfaction.

ACTIVITY 21
NEGOTIATING PRIORITIES

'When we moan about the workload, our senior officer just says, "Well, set some priorities".
Everything seems to be top priority, and it will get worse with the new government legislation, so I
don't have a clue what to do about it. The team's morale is really low because there seems
no way out.'

Aim

to provide a framework within which a team can negotiate conflicting priorities. (This activity needs a team of at least nine.)

Timing

1-2 hours
10 minutes working individually
20 minutes working in threes or fours
20-30 minutes in large group
10-60 minutes for discussion in group

Resources needed

room large enough for everyone to be working in groups of three or four at the same time without seriously disturbing each other;
tables and chairs; paper and pens;
facilitator to keep time and lead discussion

—— BRIEFING ——

1 The issues/tasks/objectives that need prioritising are listed on a sheet of paper and all participants are given a copy. (10+ issues are optimum).

2 Each participant takes 10 minutes to rank order the four issues/tasks/objectives to which they feel the team should give priority.

3 Groups of three or four individuals are given the task of reaching agreement on a common list of four issues for their group.

4 Each group then elects a delegate who meets with the other delegates. They form a group and sit in the middle of the room. Their job is to negotiate the four priorities for the agency, organisation or team. They are given 20–30 minutes.

All other participants are allowed to watch, heckle, make comments, but not to participate in the discussion.

5 The facilitator gives the entire team 10-60 minutes to reflect on how satisfied they are with the final decision of the negotiating group and on how well or not they worked together, both in smaller groups and for those in the negotiating group.

6 Before ending the session, the team should agree any action necessary, who will do it, and by when.

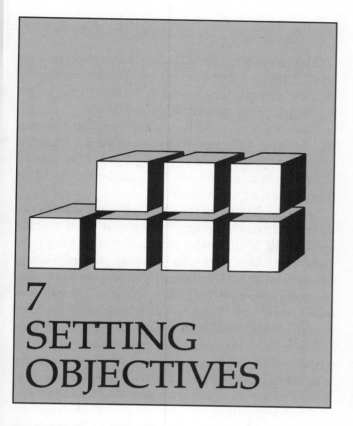

7
SETTING OBJECTIVES

Objectives are developments of your aims. They are the bridge between your vision, your values and your aims and what you will actually be doing day to day. Work without objectives is like a golf course without the holes.

A good objective should tell you what the point is of your action and how it fits in with everything else you and others are doing. It expresses concretely, but not in detailed tasks, what you are aiming to accomplish. Objectives are one stage more specific than the statement of your aims. They express the point of activities, not the activities themselves. We cannot stress how important this stage is:

- for helping each individual worker to know precisely what their own work target is, and why and how it fits into the whole;
- for giving you information on how to be more rigorous about where your time goes;
- for providing a public, agreed and clear basis for monitoring, for individual appraisal, and for evaluation.

The group of friends had reached the point of clarifying their aims. They had come to terms with their children's needs and their financial constraints, with when they could get time off work and where to go for the most likely chance of sunshine. They had eliminated the fantasy about two weeks in the Seychelles but recognised that they all wanted to go abroad. Now was the moment to get down to detailed planning.

'We (nine adults and seven children) decided we wanted to go France for 10 days together between 20 and 30 August and stay on a 4-star campsite in Vendee. The campsite should have electricity, a swimming pool, play facilities, a takeaway restaurant, a supermarket and should be within a quarter mile of the beach.

'We decided that costs, excluding spending money, should be less than £300 per family. Although economy was a priority, skimping was not. We finally agreed we preferred a 4-star campsite rather than a more basic site plus hire of a sailing boat. Those who felt passionately about the boat would rent one for odd days'.

The above two paragraphs are the 'objectives' of the holiday-makers. They express all the points wanted from the holiday, other than enjoyment, and become the focus from which organisation will subsequently stem.

This group of friends have now committed themselves without falling into the most common trap at this stage, that of getting the holiday organised without having identified clearly the end result they were seeking.

A lot of things would have to be done to get them all across the Channel in August, activities ranging from booking tickets to getting equipment and clothes, but these were only the means to achieving their objective, a holiday on a campsite in France.

The distinction between objectives and activities is crucial. It would be easy to get caught up in doing things and lose the point of it. For instance, Jean's husband Jim is a keen camper. Raj, Bhavna and their children have never been camping before. He has offered to take them camping one weekend so that they can gain some experience and confidence before the holiday. With Jim's enthusiasm, they might find themselves committed every weekend to camping practice until someone says, 'Hang on, what are we doing up to our knees in muck and cold for the fourth weekend running when we wanted warmth and sunshine?'

An example of an organisation which confused objectives and activities and lost its way is one we have worked with whose aim was to reduce isolation among elderly people. In fact, it ended up taking delinquent youngsters on holiday to Spain to increase their social skills.

You may be asking, 'How is this linked to reducing isolation among elderly people?' What happened was that this organisation started off by training young people to help the elderly. Because it had a huge influx of money and therefore could recruit a great many additional staff, it happened to recruit staff who were more interested in training young people than in helping the elderly. People forgot what the organisation had been there for in the first place.

We will again use of the example of the project for the frail elderly to illustrate how objectives fit into the planning scheme of things:

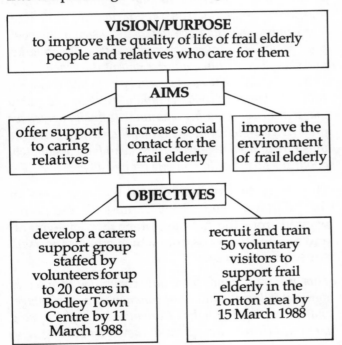

Although the process seems straightforward when stated in a diagram, it should not surprise you to know that this will seldom be the case. From each aim you have set will come a number of objectives that become the target for that achievement. In the example above these will need to include not only objectives focused on the user, such as 'to develop a carer's support group' but also objectives that are internal to the team. For example, if this organisation is moving from a direct service to the frail elderly to a training support role for volunteers, many of its workers may feel, and be, lacking in some of the training and support skills needed. They may need to develop new skills or face the fact of redundancy. Therefore another aim may need to be added to those of 'offer support to caring relatives' and 'increase social contact for frail

elderly'. It would be: 'develop staff skills to meet new aims'.

Objectives soon breed sub-objectives, which are again different from activities. 'Develop a carer's support group', may have as sub-objectives, 'locate funding', 'identify staff skills and time'.

The setting of objectives is another step in facing reality. You will need to ask how your own team resources, time, money, energy, and commitment match up to what you would like to be able to do, or feel you are expected to do.

Setting objectives is about pinning yourselves down – through being *precise* about what you intend to do. That is why it is not enough simply to state the objectives. An integral part of setting objectives is how to identify that you have successfully accomplished them. What will things look like, how will they be different, if you have accomplished what you set out to achieve? Sometimes this is relatively straightforward, 'a carers' group will meet regularly with at least 10 carers attending'. For others, particularly in areas that have to do with interpersonal skills, it can be more difficult but equally important, to establish agreed indicators of success. In a project to help young people develop their social skills, their increasing contributions in group meetings might be such an indicator.

The final aspect of pinning yourselves down in the setting of objectives is establishing realistic dates for reviewing progress and target dates for completion.

This process may lead you to get cold feet. Although you felt clear about an aim at the beginning, you may have gone through the process and reached the end with the sense that something is not quite right, or even acutely uncomfortable. You may also have found that your aim was not your real aim at all, or that you will have to add some more difficult aims to achieve the first one. For example, one organisation discovered that 'if we are going to do this we have to take the borough council with us. Its view of us will certainly have to change to make that possible.' Doing something about their relationship to the borough council became another aim.

At the end of this stage, if you still come out with clear objectives and any relevant sub-objectives, you can move on to the next step. You will be ready to estimate your time and allocate the tasks involved to go into action. However, if you have not been able to get your objectives clear, there is no point in going ahead. Your work will prove unfocused or diffuse.

You may need to restate your aim and its objectives. You may find it helpful to break it into component parts if needed. But it you feel really blocked, it may be wise to go straight away to **Activity 25,** to look at why, and through that, to see what to do.

Even if you have completed this stage to your satisfaction as a team, there may be other barriers to implementing your objectives. Something in the politics of the organisation or the community, or in the Government of the day, may make the objective impractical or unobtainable at this point in time.

Again, you will have saved yourselves an immense amount of time and resources by facing that reality at this stage. As in snakes and ladders, you will need to return to the beginning and start all over again with your aims.

ACTIVITIES

Setting objectives is a skill that improves with practice. **Activity 22: Setting Objectives** offers a framework that should help you to be rigorous about this task.

Having set what you thought were clear objectives in relation to one of your aims, you may discover that something hurts. **Activity 23: Do You Really Want To Do This?** is designed to help you face the realities of a good idea by asking yourselves whether, after all, you want to, can or should continue along this route.

Activity 24: Reality Checks may help you to look at the effect that undertaking these objectives may have on other aspects of your work or other relationships at work.

If you are clear that you do want to proceed, **Activity 25: Analysing Change** offers an approach to measuring the forces of support or resistance which you will face. It will enable you to identify these forces, measure them from your point of view, and decide what to do about them.

Activity 26: Managing Change gives guidelines to help you plan change in a productive way.

DEALING WITH COMMON PITFALLS

The closer we get to stating exactly what we want to do and why, and committing ourselves to it, the stronger seem the forces of resistance or enthusiasm. The only antidote to either is a strong dose of honesty and reality. The pitfalls reflect facets of this issue:

Measuring is anti-human
A great deal of resistance in work that involves services to people comes from people who say that tightening up statements of what you intend to do is anti-human and anti-caring, not to say simply impossible. We believe that clarity over what you intend to do allows you to be *more* human and caring in your service, not less. People need to be encouraged, however, to find a balance between clarity and flexibility, being caring enough to leave some loose ends.

Remembering to refer back
Objectives can easily be disconnected from your vision and values. Only by consistently going back and forth to check whether they still relate will you keep them connected. For example, the organisation working with the frail elderly has set as an objective developing a carers' support group with volunteers. They may need to check back to their values and ask whether this is consistent with their feelings about the use of volunteers. Is there anything that points to whether volunteer expenses should be paid? Are they intending to work with multi-ethnic and separate sex groups, and if so, do they intend to recruit volunteers to reflect this?

Dangers in enthusiasm
Are you so excited yourself or as a team about one area of work that you are being sidetracked by an interesting or unusually demanding cluster of objectives? Again, go back to the statement of purpose and check whether your objectives are really consistent with what you are aiming at.

Objectives as weapons
Many workers are reluctant to set objectives because they feel management will use these as weapons to impose more work or appraisal on them.

Appraisal is a fact of life. Right or wrong, it will be there. This process presents maximum *joint* opportunity to form objectives, check their clarity, and access achievability. What is at issue may be helping people to say 'no' or to be clear when they think their objectives are imposed or unreal.

Hands off attitudes

There is a fallacy that attitudes and relationships cannot be measured or set as objectives. This is the hole into which teams fall in the name of personality conflicts or scapegoating. Anything that goes on in a team is its business. It should be expressed as an objective for movement and change rather than as a personal comment or attack. Turning the outcomes of conflict or bad attitudes into objectives also offers the opportunity for change rather than impasse. Is someone not pulling his weight at work? Expressed in this way it will become the current complaint in the corridor. Instead it could be stated as a personal objective, set during appraisal or review between the worker and the manager. To state the objective fully, ask: What will improved performance look like? What will be happening that is different? Then work the answers into an **objective,** for example:

Objectives	Indicators of Success	Target Date	Review Date
1 to meet deadlines with reports	monthly log of reports submitted, with dates and reasons for any delay	end of each month	end of each month
2 to identify my training needs	a personal training programme	7.4.88	6 months

To rephrase the complaints as objectives also gives the worker in question the opportunity and the focus to do something about it. Remember – you cannot change the way someone feels or their attitude, only the way they behave towards you or the team's work.

ACTIVITY 22
SETTING OBJECTIVES

'What would be the point of golf if there were no hole to aim for?'

Aim
to provide a format for stating and recording objectives

Timing
variable

Resources needed
Enough of the **Objectives Recording Form** for both team and individual work

---
BRIEFING

This form can be used for listing objectives for a particular individual, for the team, or for the organisation. It may be particularly useful where a team is generating multiple objectives and in individual appraisal.
e.g.

Aim   to offer support to caring relatives

Objectives	Indicators of Success	Target Date	Review Date
1 Develop a carers' support group staffed by volunteers for up to 20 carers in Bodley Town Centre	at least 10 carers using the group regularly	open by 11.3.88	1st review 18.6.88
	a consistent core of volunteers helping		2nd review 22.9.88

---

1 Decide the way in which your team will set objectives, e.g. set team objectives in a team meeting, with resulting individual objectives set in meeting between manager and each individual worker.

If you are part of a large organisation, you may need to schedule your team's objective setting so that it meshes with that of teams more senior to yours. You may choose to work in this way if other teams within your organisation do not do so. You do not necessarily need others. You can add quality to your work independently, either as as team or as an individual.

If you know there are areas that are more difficult to pin down, such as in your relationships in the team, remember to translate these into objectives as well. It can be tempting simply to set objectives about the more clearly task-related areas of work.

2 Set times to meet to
- review team objectives
- review individual objectives

according to the approach you have agreed. The review needs to monitor the progress on target dates, to set new objectives if some have been achieved or have become unachievable or inappropriate.

3 It is difficult to set good objectives. It is easy to make them too vague to be useful, or unrealistic in relation to target dates or review. If they are not done adequately, you will not find them any use.

You may find it helpful to have someone else in the organisation comment on the way you are setting your objectives (the style, not necessarily the content). Alternatively, you might find it helpful to have a brief training session where you learn to set clear, realistic and rigorous objectives and to use them regularly in your work, rather than dragging them out, if you remember, at an annual review. If so, arrange who will set up a session, and by when.

OBJECTIVES RECORDING FORM			
OBJECTIVES	**INDICATORS of SUCCESS**	**TARGET DATE**	**REVIEW DATE**

For example:
– outcomes you seek
– the 'end product'
– evidence of
   changed
   behaviour
– training completed
	How will you really know if you have been successful?		In sufficient time to see & pull back from problems if encountered?

ACTIVITY 23
DO YOU REALLY WANT TO DO THIS?

'I've always talked about losing weight but never done nothing about it. Doing this exercise made me realise that deep down I prefer to stay as I am rather than change.'

Aim

to provide a method by which individuals and teams can quickly reflect on the pros and cons of a particular course of action.

Timing

30 minutes to one hour

Resources needed

chart paper and pens
facilitator to lead discussion

——— BRIEFING ———

This can be a particularly helpful exercise when as a team you have made a decision but some of you are still dragging your feet, or where the decision was arrived at easily enough but nothing seems to be happening.

1 The team agrees with the facilitator the **question** you want to discuss and the appropriate wording, e.g.

'shall we move to new offices?'

rather than

'we have decided to move to new offices. Are you for or against?'

2 The facilitator gets the team members to brainstorm their thoughts for and against the question, making sure to encourage them to include practical issues as well as personal feelings, e.g.

pros
more space to work in
modern offices

cons
further to travel to work
less friendly for our clients
I like it here

3 This process is continued for 10-15 minutes maximum. The facilitator then leads a general discussion of the issues raised.

4 At the end of the time you have agreed, a decision needs to be taken, either by consensus or by vote. The choices are:

yes, no, continue discussion at another time

ACTIVITY 24
REALITY CHECKS

'At the end of meetings, particularly if I am tired, I often take on commitments I either regret later or cannot realistically carry out. A few moments reflection at the time would have saved a lot of heartache later.'

Aim

to provide a framework in which individuals can pause before taking on new commitments

Timing

20 minutes

Resources needed

1 The team as a whole, or individual team members, need to decide when they need to pause. It can be following the taking on of new commitments or prior to agreeing who does what.

2 Form pairs, with each interviewing the other for 10 minutes, along the following lines:

a. how are you feeling at the moment? tired, energetic, bored, keen, disenchanted;

b. how will how you are feeling affect your commitment to the task you have just taken on, or to your availability for the tasks we are about to share out?

c. if you take on this new piece of work, what might you have to give up, directly or indirectly?

d. have you got the capacity within your present workload to take on this new work?

e. is there any way in which you can express the 'cost' (*non-financial*) of your taking on this new commitment?

3 The interviewer summarises the content of their conversation and offers, if necessary, to support their colleagues when work is being allocated. They may need support in saying 'no', in asking assertively for new work if they feel they are being passed over, or in renegotiating present work or timescales in order to take on a new task.

ACTIVITY 25
ANALYSING CHANGE

'If we had realised this course of action was going to cause so many ripples, I suspect we would never have started on it. At least we would have approached things a lot differently.'

Aim

to help team members identify and measure the forces of support or resistance in relation to any planned change

Timing

2 hours

Resources needed

Pro-forma for *Analysing Change,* one per person

a facilitator to take members through the steps, keep time and lead discussion

———— BRIEFING ————

This activity is adapted from a method called *force-field analysis* which was developed by Kurt Lewin to demonstrate effective and ineffective ways of achieving change.

As this activity can also be done by individuals or by two colleagues, the directions are addressed to individuals.

1. Identify your goal

Identify what you may want to change or to achieve, making sure that this is a single goal. Do not talk this through with anyone else at this stage, if you are doing this for yourself. Try to formulate your goal yourself. The danger of discussion at this stage is that you will be prematurely influenced by other people's ideas of what you should be aiming at.

If you are working as a team, the facilitator should help to identify the goal and get it agreed by everyone.

Using the pro forma printed here or working from one drawn on a flip chart, write your goal as a single sentence at the top of the sheet. In the circle on the left, give a 'snapshot' of the situation at present. In the circle on the right, note the changed situation you hope to achieve.

2 List forces supporting or resisting change

a. In the **left** column, list the forces or support for this change.
- these can be inside you, in the team or group, in the relationships you are part of, and in the history and environment of your organisation or wider society;

- list anything that will contribute towards your making this change, noting how it will contribute to the change;
- be as specific as possible and list everything you can think of.

b. In the **right** column, list all the forces that block, resist or restrain the change, remembering the same points as in a. above.

3 Analyse the strength of the forces

a. by first marking the forces according to three degrees of strength, in your assessment

mark in the left column (support) [+] [++] or [+++]

mark in the right column (resistance) [−] [−−] or [−−−]

b. then circle the ones that are the strongest indicators on both sides.

4. Weaken the negatives and strengthen the positives

The approach suggests that in making your chances of success greater you need to concentrate not only on strengthening the positive factors but also on weakening the negative ones.

You may find it helpful to work with a partner at this stage, for suggestions and feedback.

a. take each important negative in turn and note ways in which you could lessen the block or resistance. If you feel that there are any that you really cannot find a way of lessening at this point, write 'no action seems possible';

b. take each important positive in turn and note ways in which you can increase these sources of support.

5. Double check

- when you have completed your first analysis, go back and check what you feel about the change you first identified. Do you still want to make the change? Do you feel that you can? By when?
- If so, make a list of definite steps you will take and set yourself a deadline for each of them.
- Then subject your list to **Activity 33: Foul-Up Factors.** This test helps you ask, 'what might I do to make sure I won't actually manage to do this?'
- If you no longer feel you can or want to make the change, look at whether you want to change anything at all or just drop it. Why?

USING FORCEFIELD ANALYSIS
for personal change

write a one line summary of the change you want to make:

To _____
_____

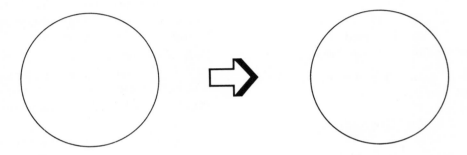

present situation   intended situation

Forces Supporting	Forces Restraining/Blocking

inside me

**in groups
and relationships**

**in my organisational,
social, political
environment**

ACTIVITY 26
MANAGING CHANGE

'The concept was excellent, but it all happened so fast that we felt destabilised and services got worse instead of better.'

Aim

to present guidelines for managing change, for the use of teams or individuals when planning organisational change

Timing

variable

Resources needed

handout, **Managing Change**

BRIEFING

Read handout and if helpful, discuss in team prior to planning change.

MANAGING CHANGE HANDOUT

1 When you are consulting about change, separate
- explaining the facts
- hearing opinions
- making decisions

e.g. (i) give people the facts first and having given them time to digest them:
(ii) listen carefully to opinions; then
(iii) on a separate occasion make a decision.

What normally happens is that people muddle the process up or try to do all three tasks at once.

2 Set clear criteria for the outcomes of the change, understanding if you can the full implications of change.

3 Although doing things more slowly is ideal, sometimes speed is essential to reduce anxiety and worry. The size and complexity of the change are important ingredients in deciding how fast and how soon.

4 Go into any planning for change with trust in the consultation process and in the general good will which most staff bring if adequately involved and informed. If you do not do this, the resulting aggression may sink your plans.

5 Issues of change involve people's feelings as well as the practical issues. Recognise and legitimise this through making opportunities in meetings and in personal discussion to face such facts.

6 Be relaxed about the process of change. If you accept it as an integral part of what you expect from work, you may find the process less painful. Do not be afraid to take the time to stop and reflect if things get really chaotic or you feel you, and/or your team, are losing your sense of perspective.

8
GETTING ORGANISED AND STAYING ORGANISED

Planning has reached the stage of sorting out who does what. The way in which you do this together and how you monitor everyone's progress will affect the success of your plans.

Had any of the families or couples been going on holiday on their own, they might have managed to get everything done by just keeping lists in their heads. But for the nine adults and seven children, as Jean pointed out, 'it was no good having all these bright ideas if we weren't going to get on with it.

'And I wasn't willing to be the group nag, hassling people to do this or that. I did insist that we meet at our house and write down all our chores on something more permanent than a beer mat. I didn't want a foul up about something everyone swore someone else had taken responsibility for one night in the pub. I brought out some paper and we listed what needed to get done. We couldn't believe how many things there were. Then we just went through and volunteered who would do what and set deadlines for both tasks and money.

'When we were volunteering, we found we had to keep quite an eye on each other. I noticed that whenever no one said, "I'll do that", one of the women would jump in and volunteer. Nick kept particularly quiet. I caught Jim volunteering to run the practice camp one weekend in March when he would already have been working three weekends on the trot.

'I've seen lists go yellow before some people get round to doing things, so I insisted on a double-check at our weekly meetings. Good thing I did, too. It is a bit of a joke amongst us that Geoff gets his mouth in gear but not much else, and we discovered that he had not got round to booking the campsite. We gave him so much stick that he checked the next morning, only to find that our first choice was already fully booked. Lucky for him that our second choice was available.'

In the middle of this Jean herself had to fly to Ireland suddenly because her mother was seriously ill. The others knew from the list what jobs she was doing and could carry on. The group faced a difficulty when Geoff discovered that the ferry prices had gone up. Most people were able to find the extra money, but Naomi and Winston who were stretched anyway, decided they simply couldn't deal with the extra, so the others had to share out their responsibilities and juggle plans a bit.

If you are trying to plan co-operatively, you need a *public* way of showing who does what and by when. This needs to be done as simply as possible while giving everyone the information they need. At the most basic level, the minutes of your meetings can either help or hinder. People who take voluminous minutes often lose points for action amidst all the words.

For some teams, or for some tasks, a simple list or *group memo* can be kept. Remember the organisation working with the frail elderly and those who care for them? Here is an example of a group memo for one of their projects.

GROUP MEMO	Dated *10.10.87*		Co-ordinator *GG*
Project: Carers Support Group		**Starting Date** *11.4.88*	
KEY TASKS		**DEADLINE**	**STAFF**
1 Review this year's budget to check available funds.		11.11.87	GG
2 Seek management committee approval for the project.		12.11.87	BW
3 Contact carers who have already shown interest and write article for next newsletter		1.2.88	CW
4 Advertise for, recruit and train volunteers		1.3.88	UH
5 Find and rent premises		1.3.88	AW
6 Apply to bottle trust for continuation funds for 89/90		28.3.88	DB

A map that is more visual, yet still simple, can give you further information. A *group project planner* can reflect not just the deadlines but the sequences in which tasks need to be done, the number of weeks over which the activity will be spread, and the interrelationship between the tasks. This means, for example, that if someone has missed a deadline or something has happened to set your schedule back, then your map can be altered to reflect the new reality. The group memo for the carers' support group project could be translated in a group project planner in the following way:

GROUP PROJECT PLANNER

TASK & DEADLINES	OCT	NOV	DEC	JAN	FEB	MAR	APRIL
1 REVIEW BUDGETS 11.11.87 GG	*						
2 MANAGEMENT COMMITTEE APPROVAL 12.11.87 BW		*					
3 CONTACT CARERS ARTICLE FOR NEWSLETTER 1.2.88 CW			S———	8	———F		
4 ADVERTISE, RECRUIT AND TRAIN VOLUNTEERS 1.3.88 UH		S———	4			———F	
5 FIND AND RENT PREMISES 1.3.88 AW	S———		18			———F	
6 APPLY FOR CONTINUATION FUNDING 28.3.88 DB					S———	6 ——F	
7 PROJECT STARTS 11.4.88							*

S = Start work on activity   **F** = Finish work on activity
* = Key date   **8** = No. of weeks from start of activity until finish

The group project planner makes it much easier to identify whether there are likely to be problems over the Christmas period or to see what happens if people take extra leave. This is a team map, but from it each individual could easily make their own project planners.

It does not matter which of these methods your team uses, as long as you are using something that will help you not only to get organised but to stay organised. Seldom if ever do plans work out straightforwardly. Being organised in this way means being organised to deal flexibly with the inevitable changes and crises which will affect your plans.

WHEN IS MY TEA BREAK?

Once you are organised you need to stay organised. Someone needs to keep an overall check on whether individuals are meeting their deadlines and to bring to the team's attention any hiccups. The co-ordinator or progress chaser in most teams may be the manager; alternatively, you may decide to ask different individuals to be the progress chasers for different projects or aspects of the work. The progress chaser also needs a progress chaser him or herself, as this example shows:

'It was my first year managing this team, so I had been very careful to make a chart of what each of us had to do to get the projects for teenagers going. The absolutely central task was getting the part-time tutors. I had agreed a date with my head of department for the advertisements to be in, and all our other plans, people for the interview panel, induction and training, school visits, you name it, were geared to this date. I turned the advertisement in to him in plenty of time, and come the Friday for the advertisement to appear, it wasn't there. I was both puzzled and devastated, and only after a lot of innocent pushing did I discover that he had simply left it lying at the bottom of his in-tray.'

Just before you start sharing out tasks and responsibilities you may want to check whether what you are trying to do still seems feasible. You may also want to ask whether there might be a different way to tackle the task. Reality needs checking and rechecking. **Activity 27: Double Checking** offers an opportunity to test for reality again.

If the way in which you have been taking minutes is not helping you to get organised **Activity 28: Taking Action Minutes** provides a pro forma for keeping minutes in a way that records the action necessary and by when.

The next two activities offer different ways of organising yourselves co-operatively and publicly. **Activity 29: Group Memo Form** gives a format for making a basic list of tasks, deadlines and persons responsible for each task. **Activity 30: Group Project Planner** presents guidelines for designing and using a planner which shows the sequences and relationships of tasks.

Often at this stage people will suddenly begin to feel nervous and wonder, 'can we manage this?' A good check to do at this point is **Activity 30: Estimating Time.** You may also want to refer back to the results of **Activity 3: Your Working Week** to see how that information relates to your new responsibilities.

Perhaps you could look at how your new choice of direction will affect other things. **Activity 23: Reality Checks** may give another way of uncovering anything you feel is not realistic.

Sharing out responsibilities will seldom be straightforward. Some members of the team more than others may be saying. 'I should do this' or 'I guess I have to do that'. When 'shoulds' and 'oughts' and 'musts' become noticeable at this stage, you need to stop and look at what is going on. **Activity 31: Being Responsible for What You Say** can be a useful way of unravelling pressures that are blocking any of you.

Activity 33: Foul-Up Factors may help you to identify things that might go wrong, many of which are not as unexpected as we think, and to decide jointly how to handle things that change our neat and tidy plans.

DEALING WITH COMMON PITFALLS

Tablets of stone syndrome

The work can look so impressive, or just so complete, to the point that you are afraid to listen to that voice that says something is not quite right. That is the reason for the number of checks built into this process. If it feels as if an objective needs restating or a deadline needs changing to be more realistic, do not be afraid to do this. Otherwise, people will begin to ignore the memo or planner because it does not really reflect what is going on. Remember, too, that if you individually are saying this, it is unlikely that you are alone. Courage in raising misgivings may be met with a sigh of relief from others who had not yet felt able to speak.

Fear of fixed plans

Much work involves crises that cannot be foreseen for tomorrow, much less in three months' time. For instance, one social services team has found itself dealing this year with more child abuse cases each week than it dealt with in the whole of last year. Having clarified together their team's purpose, aims and objectives, they are now able, quickly, to look at the consequences of this unexpected workload and to make the necessary adjustments. As a result, they are able to manage the crisis rather than fall victims to it.

Lack of reality

In editing a text, it is common to miss the same mistake again and again. In planning your work, it is possible to leave something out and have no one in the team pick it up. It can help you to have someone from outside the team look at your chart or list. You may be surprised how quickly they see the logical inconsistencies or glaring omissions.

Tricks of time

Time is not what it seems. A few things are fixed, like the dates for applying for a grant (though always double-check these, too) or sending out tenants' housing benefit giros (an inflexible deadline that itself gets missed sometimes). In other ways, time is often the scapegoat for our sense of guilt and unreality. By this stage in the process, some of those knots of unreality should have been unravelled a bit. Nevertheless, double-check whenever you hear someone or yourself saying, 'I don't have time' or alternatively, 'of course I have time'.

People are perpetually unrealistic. Many people will hate this stage and will resort to rationalisations and feeling guilty, either for what they want to do or do not want to do: 'my granny used to work hard day and night . . .'; 'if we're really committed . . .'

These should be resisted. Success and innovations have often happened at the cost of burnout, breakdowns, destruction of relationships and families, which of course the public never see. It may seem boring to work in this relentlessly revealing way, but it can work out in better service to users and greater satisfaction for workers.

People are particularly unrealistic at this stage about their own work. It can be good to have your estimates checked by someone who knows you well but is not prepared to let you get away with kidding yourself.

Can a leopard change its spots?

We are not suggesting that you quit a lifetime's habit of overwork, or guaranteeing that this way of planning can do that for you. Your priorities, for example your commitment to a particular project or the fact that you are new to a difficult job, may lead you to choose to override some of the cautions and guidelines we have offered here. At least you may be more aware of the choices you are making. Perhaps some of these reality testing tools will make your overwork less stressful.

It is possible to work hard for very long hours for short periods. If you feel the need to do this, you may want to think about when you will make the time for rest or for your holidays. The bottom line is that you can keep going on override for a while, but that if you consistently ignore the cost to yourself, at some point you may not be able to carry on. You ignore this whole issue at your peril, and therefore risk the work to which you are committed as well.

And what about people who seem to be working hard but in fact are not? The rigour and clarity of this process will also leave you as a team clearer about those who seem very busy but in fact are not pulling their weight. What you do about this depends on the culture and constraints of your organisation. There is little you can do about it without a clear policy and willingness to back it up from the highest level. Being realistic about that can itself remove fantasies and stress from your teamwork.

ACTIVITY 27
DOUBLE-CHECKING

'I remember a door-to-door salesman convincing me that I needed a brand new £4000 kitchen. Fortunately the contract allowed a get-out clause because the next day I realised that this was the last thing I wanted.'

Aim

to help individuals and teams pause before finalising important decisions

Timing

20 minutes

Resources needed

BRIEFING

1 Before you finalise very important decisions, **stop.** Take a 20 minute break. Take time individually or in pairs to reflect quietly on the decision.

Trust your inner feelings at this feelings at this stage.

2 Check particularly that what you are intending to do is still congruent with the organisation's vision and values and that the timescale has a sense of reality about it.

3 If necessary, defer the final decision for 24 hours.

ACTIVITY 28
TAKING ACTION MINUTES

'This would have been a great conference if someone had not forgotten to arrange for the bar to be open in the evenings.'

Aim
to provide a simple *aide memoire* for recording action points arising from meetings

Timing
variable

Resources needed
a copy of the **Taking Action Minutes** form

——— BRIEFING ———

This form can provide an economical alternative to detailed minutes of meetings, as well as saving valuable secretarial time.

One member of the meeting is asked to record main items under discussion and who agreed to do what by when. This can be made easier if the chairperson or facilitator states the topic, decisions and points for action at the end of each item.

The sheet can be photocopied and circulated at the end of the meeting.

Simple really.

Except it is amazing how often we do not do these simple things, leaving verbal agreements to get lost in individual memory banks.

ACTION MINUTES				
MEETING_____ DATE_____				
ATTENDED_____ APOLOGIES_____				
Agenda Item	Item Under Discussion	Action	By Whom	Deadline

ACTIVITY 29
GROUP MEMO FORM

'The best disasters usually start with confused messages about who said they would do what by when.'

Aim

to provide a format for teams to record who is responsible for what

Timing

variable

Resources needed

the **Group Memo** form or a large whiteboard with the same headings displayed

BRIEFING

Team members use the form or format as appropriate during and after planning meetings.

If there is a space which is accessible to all members of the team, it can be helpful to leave the memo on the wall between meetings.

GROUP MEMO	DATED	REVISED	REVISED	CO-ORDINATOR/ PROGRESS CHASER
PROJECT			START DATE	REVISED
KEY TASKS			DEADLINE	STAFF MEMBER RESPONSIBLE

ACTIVITY 30
GROUP PROJECT PLANNER

'We thought we had plenty of time in which to get this project started. It was only when we looked at the implications of staff holidays, potential delays in planning permission, and the threat of strike action that we realised it was a non-starter in the original time-scale.'

Aim

to provide a visual method of planning and co-ordinating the multiple tasks necessary to carry out a project or piece of work

Timing

variable

Resources needed

copy of **Group Project Planner**
whiteboard, blackboard, or large sheets of chart paper
facilitator or team leader to chart tasks

BRIEFING

A blackboard is ideal for this exercise. You need to be able to chop and change and rub out, so do not aim to make a beautiful and permanent planner.

1 List all the tasks necessary to meet the objective. Try to list them in their logical sequence, e.g.
– review budget
– seek management committee approval
– contact carers
– write article for newsletter
– advertise for volunteers
– train volunteers
– fund and rent premises

2 Estimate how long each task will take from start to finish, e.g.
review budget:
– treasurer needs two weeks' notice
– I need one week to scrutinise
Total: 3 weeks

3 Draw a rough diagram of when these activities could take place with real dates, e.g.

JAN	FEB	MAR	APRIL	MAY	JUNE	JULY	AUG

Review
Budget

Management
Committee

Contact
Carers

Articles
for Newsletter

4 Doodle until the sequence feels comfortable.

5 Look at any possible hitches that might affect your work, e.g.
staff holidays, national holidays, other major tasks such as the annual report or doing the budget.

6 Restructure your plan to take these into account.

7 Now start to tidy up the process.

a. At the beginning of each activity put the code **(S) = start**

b. At the end of each activity, put the code **(F) = finish**

c. If there is a key date which will affect activities if not met, put an * to mark this.

d. On each line put the time you estimate from start to finish, and circle it, e.g. 8 weeks from start to finish = **(8)**.

Remember to keep the project planner flexible. It is designed to give you a quick indication of not only how one person's work relates to everybody else's but also whether a late finish for one task will affect another.

8 Record any changes regularly or the whole planner becomes useless. Arrange how to do this, e.g. at a team meeting, at a special meeting, individually; who will be responsible for co-ordinating the planner update, and when.

GROUP PROJECT PLANNER			CO-ORDINATOR/PROGRESS CHASER											
PROJECT..........................			....											
KEY TASKS	DEADLINE	STAFF MEMBER	MONTH 1	2	3	4	5	6	7	8	9	10	11	12

S = START OF ACTIVITY   * = DEADLINE
F = FINISH OF ACTIVITY   8 = NO. OF WEEKS FROM START TO FINISH OF ACTIVITY

ACTIVITY 31
ESTIMATING TIME

'When I'm happy I always underestimate the time an activity will take. When I'm tired or sad I overestimate. Therefore, usually I don't have a clue.'

Aim

to provide a quick method for estimating the number of working hours a new task or project will take

Timing

30 minutes to 1 hour

Resources needed

paper (scrap paper or old envelopes will do)
pencil or pen
facilitator to keep time, do briefing, if working in group

——— BRIEFING ———

The following is a job for using the back of an envelope: it is a scribble exercise, not a formal piece of work.

If it cannot be done fairly quickly, before you take on new commitments, then it may not be much use to you.

1 Pick one of your most simple personal or team objectives. Brainstorm all the things you would need to do to fulfil that objective.

2 Then group all these items into broad categories of things related to each other.

a. put them on a rough graph;

b. estimate the amount of time in hours that each task will take and note this down;

c. add up the columns and total.

3 Divide the total number of hours you have arrived at above by the amount of time you currently have to do this task. Assume that one working day totals 8 hours. In the example on the next page this would be approximately 23 weeks.

4 Multiply this figure by 50 per cent for errors in calculation or unforeseen problems. This will give you, in the example, approximately 35 weeks as the **shortest** amount of time the project will take.

5 Now look at any factors which may slow the process down, e.g. planning permission takes six months; there is an embargo on staff recruitment for a year.

Adjust your time-scale to arrive at a new figure for the **longest** time necessary to do this project. In our example this may now be 60 weeks.

6 Bear these factors in mind when agreeing to new work or when making promises about when a project will start or finish.

This way of quickly estimating the rough reality of the time involved could save a lot of pain in the long run.

The back of an envelope drawn below is an example of how to estimate the time involved in setting up a support group for carers of the frail elderly (described earlier in this chapter). One of the columns has been filled in in detail to illustrate how to put all your brainstormed items into broad categories.

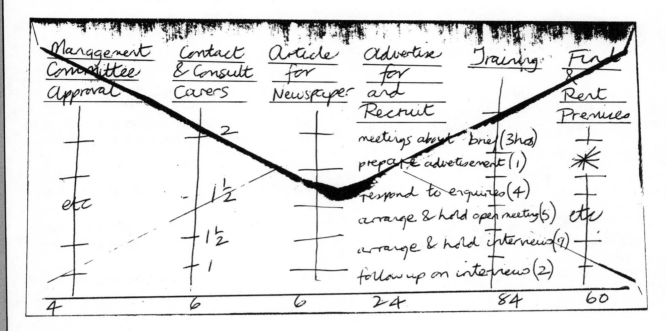

Total time: 184 hours

Average time available to work on this project:
1 day per week

Shortest overall time it will take:
184 hours ÷ 8 (no. of hours in a working day)
       = 23 weeks

Add 50% for unforeseen activities:
275 hours ÷ 8 = 35 weeks

***Longest** overall time it will take: known complicating factor – planning permission takes an average of 6 months. Therefore we have to add that time into our calculations. Under this calculation, the longest time stretch necessary for this project is now approx. 60 weeks.

ACTIVITY 32
BEING RESPONSIBLE FOR WHAT YOU SAY

'If I had had the courage to say "no" rather than "I suppose I could", I would be on holiday now. Instead I'm reviewing the organisation's accounts for a colleague who said _HE_ was too busy because of having to fit in _HIS_ holiday.'

Aim

to help you take full responsibility for the tasks you take on, rather than responding out of guilt, pressure, fear, or a sense you have no option

Timing

1 hour
30 minutes working individually
30 minutes in group discussion

Resources needed

pen and paper for each individual
a facilitator to give direction and keep time

BRIEFING

If your attempts at sharing out tasks are peppered with, 'I guess I shoulds' or 'I know I ought tos'; if you hear yourself saying, 'she has to do this', or 'I can't do that', then these exercises may help tease out some of the issues involved.

1 Each individual is asked to remember comments they have made during this meeting and/or earlier meetings and write down four or five examples of when they have said,

> 'I can't . . .'
> 'I must . . .'
> 'I have to . . .'
> 'I don't have any choice . . .'
> 'I ought to . . .'
> 'I should . . .'

e.g. 'I should meet with the head of that section next week';
'I ought to volunteer to serve on that new working party';
'I simply can't take on anything else'.

2 After 15 minutes the facilitator invites each individual to rewrite all their sentences, choosing from the following phrases, as appropriate:

> 'I choose to'
> 'I choose not to'
> 'I don't want to'
> 'I want to'

If yours is an organisation with statutory obligations, you may want to add variations such as

> 'I do not want to do this work
> although I understand by law it
> must be done.'

3 Individuals take a few minutes to reflect in pairs on what they have learned about themselves from the exercise, e.g.

> 'I keep saying, "I don't have time to
> take on anything else". I've just
> discovered that if I gave up my
> painting class and some of my time
> with the children, I would have
> time. So what I am going to try to
> say in the future is, "I am
> choosing not to take on anything else
> at present".'

4 The facilitator then leads a group discussion. Relevant issues to raise might include:

- exploring what pressures in the team or organisation's culture may be encouraging such language and behaviour;
- what people fear if they take more assertive responsibility for what they want or do not want to do;
- what the consequences would be, or are imagined to be, for the work of the team if individuals were to change their behaviour.

5 Participants are invited to make a commitment to monitoring each other's use of language in future meetings, particularly when people are volunteering, or 'being volunteered', for new tasks, e.g. requiring anyone who uses 'ought' or 'should' to rephrase the sentence before their offer is accepted.

ACTIVITY 33
FOUL-UP FACTORS

'The unexpected is usually all too predictable.'

Aim

to identify and to plan for those predictable disasters before a commitment is made to a particular set of plans

Timing

1 hour
30 minutes working individually
30 minutes working in pairs

Resources needed

none are necessary; notes of plans may be useful
a facilitator if you are doing it as a team;
a partner if you want to do it individually

BRIEFING

1 Each individual is asked to examine their own plans for a project or task and to note all the things that might go wrong with these plans, i.e.

- personal – *'I usually bite off more than I can chew.'*
- organisational – *'I know there is a bottleneck in the personnel dept.'*
- other – *'yet another government directive may force another priority.'*

2 Each individual finds a partner with whom to discuss these plans

a. to check that they still make sense;

b. to see if anything has been missed;

c. to test their partner's sense of personal and organisational reality.

3 If there is the time or inclination, individuals or the team may want to 'make a plan' about how to counteract their most habitual foul-up factor.

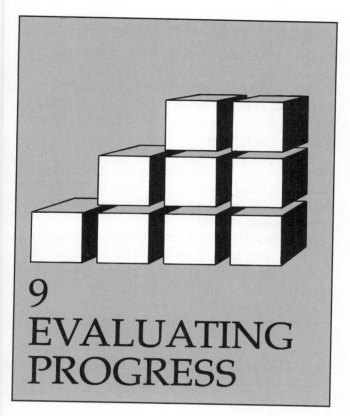

9 EVALUATING PROGRESS

Throughout the planning you will have been checking and rechecking how you are getting on, with the tasks and with each other. At an appropriate point you will need to complete the cycle with a fuller review.

Teams need to be able to answer the question, 'how are we doing?', individuals need to be able to answer the question 'how am I doing?'. Implicit in both these questions is, 'in relation to what I thought I or we were doing or should be doing'.

This is not a stage that can be left to coffee breaks or the pub. Time needs to be set aside and a framework for both team and individual reflection agreed. Reflection is fundamental to the team-

building approaches presented here, at each stage and at the end. Without this feedback, you may find yourselves just scrabbling in the dark, hitting some things wide of the mark.

Even before they went on holiday the group of friends had planned a big gathering after they returned. Each of them brought something to share for supper, plus any left-over duty free or mineral water.

'Basically what we were celebrating was that we actually did it – since several times it had felt like a close thing. We reminisced about the good things we had done and about the few disasters too. It got quite riotous at this stage, since nothing is such a relief as talking about near disasters when you have survived them.

'More seriously, this was an opportunity to say thank-you to different people who did little things that often go unnoticed. We had been upset at the time when Geoff's slowness meant we lost our first-choice campsite. As it was, the second choice turned out to be fine. But we also discovered that he had written to and investigated dozens of sites initially, even though things went a bit wrong with the booking.

'Bhavna and Raj made a special point of telling Jim how much his patience on the practice camp had helped their confidence and enjoyment of the holiday. My two teenagers were around that night and they joined in. I was touched when they thanked Sarah for taking them shopping in the nearby town one day.

'On the negative side. It was painfully clear to the rest of us, as well as to them, that one of the marriages was not working for either partner. And despite the fun we had, in the planning and the holiday, most of us admitted that it was lot of hard work, too, and that we wouldn't want to do it again next year.'

This final gathering was an important aspect of the holiday. It marked the end of the planning cycle, and left them with a sense of what they had learned and with information for the future.

Learning how to 'do evaluation' is actually learning how to be clear about what you are doing. The stages of a review or evaluation at the end of a piece of work reflect the stages of planning you have already been through.

1 Reviewing your vision. *'How did we end up doing community work with adults when we were aiming to do group work with young people?'*

2 Reviewing how, or whether, your objectives were met. In the example of the support group for carers of the frail elderly, they kept a record of how many attended and had used a questionnaire for all carers when they set up the group, which they planned to follow up. They were already monitoring how they were meeting their objective of running a group.

3 Asking how far the values, policies and strengths were kept in meeting your objectives. *'We certainly managed to open the new advice centre but yet again we have employed only white workers'. 'We have managed to reorganise from volunteers to a paid worker team, but our campaigning work has lapsed during this period.'*

4 Looking at how you got organised and stayed organised. *'Our planner has not been touched for two months and we are late again with the annual report. But everyone pulled their weight in the sponsored walk this year.'*

5 Reviewing individual contributions to the system, beginning with a self review. How did people do with the tasks they undertook and with the objectives they set themselves? *'The majority of staff not only met their objectives but managed to do so in often very difficult circumstances, e.g. after the office had been flooded and with a lot of staff sickness during the winter. One individual has presented real difficulties, missing work targets and consistently causing problems in meetings. However, he is working with an external consultant who is helping him to look at the possibilities of another career.'*

6 Asking what have you learned as individuals about yourselves. *'I have come close to burnout on several occasions and often put pride before common sense.'*

7 Reflections on what it all adds up to, individually and collectively. *'This had been a difficult and challenging project. We've succeeded because of the energy and creativity of a large number of people. However, most of us feel like a rest and would not want to repeat the experience in the near future.'*

8 Considering where you go next. *'We need to plan carefully the introduction of new staff over the next 18 months, since several of us have indicated we are looking for new jobs. We need to do this so that those of us who want to leave can move on without feeling guilty.'*

This is essentially a review and evaluation tool for you as a team. It should improve the quality of your teamwork and your services. It lays the foundation for any appraisal or evaluation scheme by giving you the information about how you as individuals and as a team are getting on.

This should enable you to make a case to funders or to senior officers when appropriate, or to brief an outside evaluator. Whatever the external demands for evaluation, whether from your managing committee or the DHSS, a process in which review is integral will leave you prepared for it. Seeing the review as part of planning and getting on with the task should help you avoid the state of defensiveness that characterises many teams when they are having evaluation or appraisal 'done to' them.

ACTIVITIES

Review is built into each stage of this planning process. In order to bring these together more explicitly, **Activity 34: Are We on The Right Track?** helps you to agree the kinds of things it might be useful to monitor and gives you a checklist of ways of going about these.

Reviewing will be of limited use if you are not able to be open with each other about what is going badly and what is going well. **Activity 35: Positive Feedback** offers a way of treating each other with openness and respect.

Activity 36: Sorting Out Differences should help you deal with any differences which have arisen.

Reviewing at the end of a piece of work often overlaps taking stock in preparation for work. Many of the activities in **Chapter 3: Taking Stock** may be appropriate for you to use at this stage.

DEALING WITH COMMON PITFALLS

Counting what?
The counting approach to answering the question, 'how are we doing?' needs to be examined sceptically. Do you know why you are counting? If not, find out.

'I remember being asked to count the number of kids on supervision orders in our county. Every year I would go to the conference of magistrates and probation officers and say either "supervision orders are up 20 per cent" to which they would all answer "good, excellent". Or I would say, "supervision orders are down 20 per cent", to which they would all answer "good, excellent". The point was, none of us had a framework for knowing whether the figures were good or bad.'

The success syndrome
A common misconception is that if you – individually or as a team – are doing your work well from the point of view of the users, and you can prove this in evaluation, you will be secure and get kudos.

It is a home truth that, as often as not, decisions about the future of a project or a department or an area of work are based on political considerations, not primarily on good practice. Some good work gets killed off; some bad work survives. The evidence for this leaves teams with a choice of their own values: do you work to the best of your own standards for the satisfaction of the service you can give to users and the environment you can create for yourselves, for as long as you are there (while using all your political skills to survive)? Or do you join the cynics and feel put upon by the system?

Big-is-more-sophisticated

Do you think, because you are part of a large bureaucracy or commercial organisation, that this team-centred approach will not work for you? Does it seem too simple to work in such a large setting? At the end of the day, whether in a multinational or a community project, a small group of people (a team) will sit down together to make far-reaching decisions. They will decide to commit greater or lesser financial resources and more or less people to doing something to further the vision of their organisation.

Hogging information

Information is power, particularly information from the boss or major decision maker about the performance of individuals and the organisation or team. it can be tempting to keep such information centrally. It is important to avoid doing this for two reasons: first, simply to avoid overloading one person; but also, to enable the information to be used constructively so that all member of the team have a stake in the outcomes.

Cataclysm and surprise

Evaluation and appraisal have got themselves bad names as cataclysmic events which threaten terrible surprises. A team that plans its work together in this step-by-step way, whatever the levels of hierarchy which may be represented within it, is inoculating itself against such shocks. Difficulties which might build up to cataclysms, such as someone not doing parts of the job that are essential to a piece of work, can be dealt with more easily if they are faced as they arise.

ACTIVITY 34
ARE WE ON THE RIGHT TRACK?

'In reality, the practice of monitoring how things are going is comforting and rewarding. Yet it is something that we all try to avoid because we are frightened it will tell us something we do not want to know.'

Aim

to provide a checklist to help teams design their own methods of monitoring and evaluation

Timing

1-3 hours depending on team size

Resources

Monitoring and Evaluation checklist
chart paper
facilitator to lead discussion, keep time

BRIEFING

The following checklist can be used as an agenda for a meeting specifically arranged to discuss monitoring and evaluation.

MONITORING AND EVALUATION CHECKLIST

1 Has the team's 'vision' been clearly stated?
How will it be reviewed, by whom and when?

2 Have individual and team objectives been clearly stated?
How will they be reviewed, by whom and when?

3 Have our values, policies and strategies been clearly stated?
How will they be reviewed, by whom and when?

4 How well have we worked together as a team?
How can this be monitored?
How often do we need to do this?
Who will do it?

5 How efficiently do we organise ourselves:
– meetings
– finance
– planning
– staff supervision/recruitment/training and development
How can this be monitored?
How often do we need to do ths?
Who will do it?

6 How do individuals get feedback on their work, the development of their skills, their career and training needs, their general contribution to the team and the organisation?
How can this be done?
How often does this need to be done, and by whom?

7 Do we need to take time to review our feelings about each other, as they affect our work, and/or about our work?
How do we do this, who will do it, and when?

8 Do we need time to review our overall vision?
How will we do this, by when and who will help us?

ACTIVITY 35
POSITIVE FEEDBACK

'Our two senior managers had created an ugly atmosphere of competition in the team. In our meetings their feedback made it clear who got gold stars and who got told off each week. We could change their behaviour (altogether it did change gradually), but we finally got together ourselves. We talked together about how to respond to them assertively rather than in kind and I how to give assertive feedback to each other.'

Aims
to provide guidelines for giving and receiving feedback as a basis for team discussions
to provide a team with the basis for designing their own guidelines for feedback.

Resources needed
Handout on **Positive Feedback**
chart paper and pens (optional)
facilitator (optional)

Giving and Receiving Feedback

Basic Values:
- treat and expect to be treated with respect: be soft on the person and hard on the problem
- be genuine
- remember a compliment or criticism is as much about the giver as the given to

Guidelines

Giving:
- Do not say: '[positive feedback] **but** [critical feedback]'
  insteads say: '[positive] **and** [critical]'
  e.g. *'I really appreciated how skilfully you chaired our staff meetings, and I still wish you could get to them on time!'*
- Be specific: state what happened before you go on to say what you feel and/or want
- pay attention to body language
- judge the situation: choose your time

Receiving:
- accept my comment first, only then elaborate
- give credence to what has been said even if you do not agree
- ask for details if the person is not specific enough
- accept any 'facts' without taking on any putdowns

Follow through: make sure the feedback is
- understood
- accepted
- any action agreed

The final stage moves from the *telling* of feedback, through *asking* if it is understood and accepting, to *negotiating* and *agreeing* any action that may be appropriate.

BRIEFING

1 Participants are given the handout to read prior to a session where feedback is going to take place
or

2 The handout is used as a basis for group discussion about good feedback. The team may then want to add to these guidelines or to devise its own list.

3 Team members agree ways in which they can practise more effective feedback and how they will monitor their behaviour.

ACTIVITY 36
SORTING OUT DIFFERENCES

'I had felt nobody in the group liked me. It was such a relief to realise they simply wanted me to stop smoking in our meetings and that otherwise my contribution was valued. I wish someone had said something earlier.'

Aim

to provide a model form as a basis for negotiating changes in behaviour between team members

Timing

30 minutes – 2 hours
10-30 minutes individually
20 minutes-1½ hours in pairs and group

Resources needed

the model form **Sorting Out Differences**
a facilitator to lead discussion if the model form is used in a group

—————— BRIEFING ——————

1 This may be used as a basis for individuals to sort out minor differences, e.g.
'It would help me concentrate in training sessions if you
a. gave me feedback *more* often
b. smoked *less* often
c. but *continued* bringing me coffee when you see I'm sagging'.
It is important that people writing their messages be as specific as possible or give examples.

2 Teams may wish to use this activity as part of team review. In this case it is important that everyone in the team sends everyone else a message.

3 If teams use the forms, time needs to be set aside so that individuals may meet in pairs to discuss the implications of what has been written. Individuals may wish to look for some compromise, ask for clarification or explain why they do not agree with the perspective of the message-sender.

4 In a large organisation, this approach can be helpful for teams at different levels within the hierarchy to send messages to each other as part of each team's review. The contents of the messages can then be included in each team's meetings, and a message returned after discussion.

If it is used in this way, it must not be seen as a substitute for face-to-face meetings, but as an additional aid for teams at all levels to communicate with each other. It is specially important that particular examples accompany each message.

Generalisations do not offer enough information to enable a person or group receiving the message to negotiate changes.

Sorting Out Differences

To:

_____

From:

_____

It would help me to

if you were to do:

MORE OF

LESS OF

However, please continue to do the following in the same way

(In each section above be specific, frank but not judgemental, and give an example of each.)

POSTSCRIPT

HEALTH WARNINGS: PERSONAL SURVIVAL

The model of planning described in the previous chapters is relatively straightforward. Life is not. You may have reached this point still feeling unhappy, anxious, angry or stressed about your work.

The reasons for how you are feeling may be personal, may lie in your team or organisation, or in outside political, social or economic circumstances.

Whatever the circumstances each of us is ultimately responsible for looking after ourselves and for how we feel. This is something that many of us tend to forget.

There is very little that can be identified as being wholly external or a wholly personal factor. In some political contexts, certain social and cultural environments, and selected organisations the destructive pressure is enormous and belongs entirely to those factors. It is vitally important that workers and teams have the opportunity to understand this and to place the responsibility for these pressures in the right place rather than, as often happens, blaming yourselves for the failures, inconsistencies and inequalities of the system. Sometimes doing this may be enough to make the work tolerable. On occasion it may be necessary to leave a job to prevent total disenchantment, burnout or breakdown.

Nevertheless, if you go through this planning process and the work still does not feel right, there is a reasonable chance that the problem lies inside, not outside yourself.

'I have been blaming my boss for giving me too much work for years and also for going behind my back to find our what was going on in my department. It has been quite a shock to realise that I have been overworking as a way of avoiding problems at home. And one of the results of the overload I have created is that I have not had enough time to support my staff adequately.'

It may be that different aspects of your personality have very different ideas about how you should be running your life. For example, an activity overload is not just about bad planning; it can be about your own need to work in that way. It may be positive: it gives you kicks, excitement, stimulus, fun, friends. Or it may be negative: perhaps to avoid facing issues that are less immediately rewarding, whether these are tasks like planning or administration or a relationship at home or at work that is on rocky ground.

Other areas where personal issues can confuse and complicate issues at work are:

the assertion problem. You do not have the confidence to say clearly what you want so you are taking on things you do not want to do, missing out those you would like and feeling that you are not making your best contribution. You may have spells of feeling it was a mistake to take you on. It may help to ask for time with your senior to work out your job more clearly, or to do a course in confidence or assertiveness training.

the problem of not knowing what you want. You may not be wholly aware of your personal needs in work, so that they only emerge in a roundabout way. You may feel uncomfortable with proposals others make without knowing quite why, or what to suggest as an alternative. For example, having felt that this is not the right time for a consultative group meeting you finally discover that you are simply feeling overloaded with working in groups.

unfinished business. Often individuals or teams leave arguments, conflicts or disappointments unresolved. This blockage is likely to affect your planning discussions and your teamwork generally, until you do something about it.

hooked into reaction. You may find yourself having such strong feelings about some person or some issue, that you react emotionally whenever you have to deal with them. You probably cannot see any good in what this person does, no reason why they are in the job, nor anything they have to offer. Such extreme emotion about a person or an issue should be a warning sign that something inside yourself is out of balance. However righteous you feel about the issue or the person, you may need to recognise that you are playing some part in making the situation worse.

'I'd rather be somewhere else . . .' If you are tired or have pressing problems at work or at home, it can be difficult to give your attention to planning. If this is the case for you or for others in the team, it can be worth spending time at the beginning of a session on an exercise where you imagine the pressures, load them into a suitcase, and leave them outside the door until after the meeting. Alternatively, you may want to ask for the meeting to be postponed, if you sense it is badly timed, not only for you but for other members of the team.

facing a career crossroads. People at a career crossroads are very often ambivalent about taking on any new commitments at work, or even discussing the future. It may be that everyone in the team needs some time to talk about people's career needs and stages, and that these need to be taken into account in planning.

personal priorities. Sometimes your own needs may become greater than those of the organisation, e.g. there may be particular problems at home, or you have just had a baby, or you have reached the point where your leisure time is more important than the habit you have had of working overtime. The more openly these needs are acknowledged and handled sensitively, the better.

As a member of the team, you can say you need less stress at work because you have personal pressures, without needing to say why. There may be an issue here about home life and work life the whole team may need to face. Is pressure being put on people to work hours for which they are not contracted, and therefore building up unacknowledged conflicts between those who give priority to their personal commitments and those who at this point are willing to work all hours?

WHAT CAN YOU DO?

The most important first step is to recognise that you need to do something for yourself. You may want to take action on one or more levels, in your team, your organisation, or personally outside working hours.

Although staff are an organisation's most important resource, many organisations do not yet have an adequate framework for supporting and supervising individuals. The aim of such a framework is to help each individual worker to stay effective.

Support and supervision
The key elements of a framework for support and supervision are valid whether you work in a hierarchy, or in a collective or non-hierarchical setting. These are:

- that the tasks involved in the work are clearly described in the form of accurate and meaningful job descriptions;
- that roles within your team are clear: that you each know who is accountable for making sure work is done and who is responsible for carrying out particular tasks;
- that some sort of framework is agreed for workload management, i.e. that the tasks people are given are possible to achieve within a normal working week, and that a regular review and monitoring system is set up with colleagues or with a supervisor to check on progress so that workloads can be adjusted;
- that time is set aside every few months, whether for individuals and/or as a team, to give feedback on each worker's performance, using criteria and indicators that have been agreed in advance with each member of staff;
- that enough time is given for basic training, orientation and induction for new jobs or tasks and that individuals are not being asked to do things they are not competent to perform;
- that there is time for individuals to talk about personal feelings, aspirations, ambitions, and that some way exists of measuring how these are being met;
- that a culture is created where the team is sensitive to the effect of such personal issues as bereavement or separation on an individual's capacity to work, without intruding on their privacy.

Personal options

There may be reasons why you cannot get or use the support and supervision suggested in these points. You may be in an organisation that does not provide a suitable framework for support and supervision to meet your needs. As an alternative you might consider paying for a professional consultation, or arranging with a trusted colleague to give mutual regular support. Or you may prefer something more personal, and entirely outside work, such as counselling or therapy.

The important point is the one made at the beginning of this postscript: **Ultimately, each of us as individuals is responsible for our personal survival and for acting from our own personal awareness, whatever the circumstances.**

In the end, an organisation may not be right for you. It is important not to let yourself feel trapped but to acknowledge your need for change.

In conclusion

It may seem that planning takes a lot of energy and reveals many problems you could have done without. But it is a bit like healthy eating: you wonder how you lived any other way for so long; and a healthier way of eating gradually becomes a habit.

You only have to get this model 50 per cent right for it to make a more than 50 per cent difference to your team and to individuals. If you are getting it 50 per cent right you are actually doing very well in comparison to most teams. More important, 50 per cent is the point when you start seeing returns for the time and energy you have invested.

You have a choice about whether to remain the victim of your work or whether to take another route. This alternative route may be no less difficult; but it will offer more rewards at the end of the day.

Further information about training based on methods outlined in this book may be obtained from the Management Unit at the National Council for Voluntary [...] ford Square, London WC1 [...]

Courses on [...] regularly by the Conferen [...] Institute for Public Administration, 3 Birdcage Walk, London SW1H 9JH (tel: 01-222 2248).

Lois Graessle
1 Magnolia Wharf
Strand on the Green
London W4 3NY England
Tel: 020 8995 0244